Believing
in
God

by
Daniel Jenkins

LAYMAN'S
THEOLOGICAL
LIBRARY

THE WESTMINSTER PRESS

PHILADELPHIA

Acknowledgment is made for permission to quote from:

Péguy and Les Cahiers, by Daniel Halévy. Longmans, Green & Company, New York and Dennis Dobson, London.

Scripture quotations from the Revised Standard Version of the Bible are copyright, 1946 and 1952, and are used by permission.

Library of Congress Catalog Card No.: 56–9576

PRINTED IN THE UNITED STATES OF AMERICA

CONTENTS

5

6 *Contents*

FOREWORD

The religious book market is full of books for " the intelligent layman." Some are an insult to his intelligence. Others are covertly written for professional theologians. A few are genuine helps in communicating the faith.

In this spate of books being thrust at the lay reader, what distinctive place can the Layman's Theological Library claim to hold? For one thing, it will try to remind the layman that he *is* a theologian. The close conjunction of the words " layman " and " theological " in the title of the series is not by chance but by design. For theology is not an irrelevant pastime of seminary professors. It is the occupation of every Christian, the moment he begins to think about, or talk about, or communicate, his Christian faith. The injunction to love God *with all his mind,* necessarily involves the layman in theology. He can never avoid theology; if he refuses to think through his faith, he simply settles for an inferior theology.

Furthermore, the Layman's Theological Library will attempt to give a *wholeness* in its presentation of the Christian faith. Its twelve volumes cover the main areas of Christian faith and practice. They are written out of similar convictions which the authors share about the uniqueness of the Christian faith. All the authors are convinced that Christian faith can be made relevant, that it can be made understandable without becoming innocuous, and that (particularly in view of the current " return to religion ") it is crucially important for the layman to

7

commit himself to more than " religion in general." The Layman's Theological Library, then, will attempt a fresh explora-
tion of the Christian faith, and what it can mean in the life of
twentieth-century man.

Believing in God poses difficulties for most people, whether
Christian or not. One of the great merits of Mr. Jenkins' book
is that he takes these difficulties seriously. He recognizes that
believing in God has always been difficult for men, and that
although our contemporary situation may seem to aggravate
the problem for us, the problem is one which men have always
had to face. After two chapters in which he faces some of
these difficulties, the author devotes his third chapter to the
affirmations which Christian faith makes about God as revealed
in Jesus Christ.

Many books stop at just that point, assuming that " faith "
will take care of the difficulties. But Mr. Jenkins points out
that to believe in the God of the Bible is to face a host of
brand-new difficulties, and in the last part of his book he comes
to grips with these.

This book, then, is designed for the person who has questions
and is willing to face them, who cares enough about answers
to do a little hard thinking with the author, and who is honest
enough to realize that although not all questions will disappear
simply by reading ninety pages, the remaining questions can
be set within a context of meaning which, while not destroying
mystery, invests the very mystery itself with new meaning.

ROBERT MCAFEE BROWN

BELIEVING
IN GOD

1

Why Is Belief in God So Difficult?

The Mystery of Life

That belief in God is so difficult," Miss Marianne Moore has said, "is apparently one of God's injustices." Whether it is an injustice or not, it is certain that most reflective people today do not find that belief in God comes easily to them.

Modern people are not peculiar in this respect. One of the most misleading assumptions that is made about belief in God is that there ever was a time when men found it really easy. But perhaps we do make it more difficult for ourselves than many other generations of people have done, because we so readily assume that it should be easy to believe in God, and that it must be God's fault if it turns out not to be.

On the seal of the Church of Scotland is a drawing of a burning bush, and the words underneath it, *nec tamen consumebatur,* "and it was not consumed," have been a favorite motto of many Presbyterian churches in this country as well. The reference, of course, is to the story of the burning bush which Moses saw when he was watching his flocks in Horeb. This story marks the beginning of the history of Israel as a distinct nation, and the burning bush is a sublime symbol of the inexhaustible vitality of God. Its purpose, like that of most of the miraculous signs in the Bible, was not so much to reveal

God as it was to attract the attention of Moses. It made him say, " I will turn aside and see this great sight, why the bush is not burnt." And we are told that it is only when the Lord sees that Moses *does* turn aside, that he speaks to him.

What was true for Moses is true for all men. God provides signs of his presence and activity, but he will not speak to men unless they turn aside to see. Belief in him is not self-evident. It demands an effort of concentrated attention. Perhaps the chief reason why we find belief difficult today is that we find it so hard, amid our many distractions, to make that kind of effort.

It is not surprising that belief in God should not be self-evident. Life in general does not carry its meaning on the surface. We must recognize, in fact, that life is a mystery. It is not mysterious simply in the sense in which a puzzle is mysterious, where once the answer is found all is clear. On the contrary, the more we are able to understand of life's meaning, the deeper does our consciousness of its mystery become. The person who is an expert on a subject is generally the one who confesses most readily how little he knows. And as our knowledge of people we love grows, we become more aware than ever of how much there still is to understand about them, and that we can never completely fathom the depths of their personal identity. The more profound the question is that we ask of life, the clearer this becomes. Mystery and meaning go together and involve each other.

A great deal of confusion has arisen because people have been reluctant to accept this mysterious character which life possesses or, when they have accepted it, have thought that belief in the Christian God did away with mystery. The view of the world that the Bible presents is not that of a floodlit stage, where all is clear and sharply defined. Rather, it is that of a world of mystery, wonderful and bewildering, where, out of darkness and shadows and confusion of tongues, a light shines and a voice speaks. The light is sufficient to illuminate our path and the voice is clear enough to give essential directions, but darkness remains around the path, and no words are wasted in trying to explain many baffling things about life. The light is one that men, having eyes, can fail to see, and, when God speaks, his voice is one that men, having ears, can fail to hear.

The Bible goes out of its way to emphasize the enigmatic character of human experience. "Watchman, what of the night?" the people anxiously cry. And the answer is often simply, "Morning comes, and also the night" (Isa. 21:11, 12). And we shall have frequently to note that nowhere else are the realities of death and evil, in all their inscrutability, brought more relentlessly before the notice of men than in the pages of this same Bible.

The New Testament speaks of the mystery of the gospel and describes it as God's wisdom in a mystery. By this the New Testament means that God's purpose is being disclosed to those who are in a position to see it, but that, because it is indeed God's secret, it is unfathomable even while disclosing meaning. We are able to observe the mystery, but not fully to understand it, because the source of meaning lies in God and not in us.

This is not to say, however, that God's self-disclosure, his revelation, is to be thought of as something irrational. God may not answer many of the questions we should like to have answered and he is greater than our understanding, but that does not mean that he cannot stand up to the scrutiny of critical reason. If he could not, our minds would be more godlike than God himself. The mystery of God is not mysterious in the sense of the weird and the occult, of those experiences which come in the twilit world of the semiconscious. God offers more to

the understanding than it can readily assimilate and set in
order, and he makes us aware of depths of meaning greater
than we are able to fathom. He is the truth and insists that he
should be received as the truth, and yet in knowing him as
the truth we discover that he is greater than our minds.

These facts of the mysterious nature both of life and of God
must be clearly grasped from the outset if the reasons for belief
in the Christian God are to be properly understood.

Religious Denials of Mystery

There can be no doubt, for example, that many thoughtful
and sensitive people have been prevented from giving serious
attention to the Christian faith because it has been presented
to them in forms that seem to drain life of its mystery. These
people are conscious of the reality of the tragic element in human experience and of the complexity of many questions of
right and wrong and they have a healthy distrust of simple
answers.

But there are many so-called " Christians " who have no patience with such hesitancy. They believe that they have a duty
to provide an answer to every question and seem to think that
the very foundations of faith are imperiled if sometimes they
have to confess that they do not know. The vigor with which
they denounce sin and evil is matched only by the assurance
with which they detect and label them. They give the impression of living in a very well-charted universe, where they are
able to keep without difficulty to the appointed way and where
they are completely at home. No disturbing fresh reality ever
breaks in to upset their composure or to revise their judgments.
God works always in obvious and calculable ways and shows
a gratifying tendency to confirm the expectations of his
servants.

Few people irritate their fellows more readily than individuals of this type. They are like the clergyman in the *New Yorker* cartoon who was looking down on his wife with an amused and complacent air while she was crying in frustration: "You have an answer for everything, haven't you?"

And although the same attitude is not so readily objectionable in institutions, it is no less prevalent and certainly no less dangerous. All churches that have a strongly consolidated institutional life and large numbers of formal adherents are open to the temptation to develop an attitude of this kind. The Roman Catholic Church provides only the most striking example of a church that has succumbed to this temptation, at least among its more official spokesmen. They give the impression of knowing more about heaven and earth than it is given to mortal men to know and of taking such knowledge for granted. As an English Roman Catholic bishop has put it: "We have the assurance of our position. We have the certainty of the possession of truth. We have the answer to all the questions." (Quoted from "The Tablet," London, July 26, 1947, by A. R. Vidler in *Christian Belief.*)

In the same way, what repels people in Protestant Fundamentalism is not merely its intellectual inconsistencies, but also its aggressive assertion, in defiance of the Book it so loudly claims to hold in reverence, that it need have no doubts about its own ability to exercise faithfully its stewardship of the mysteries of Christ. It is all in the Book, and the Book is in the pocket, to be whipped out and unreflectingly quoted when any point arises, so what is there to worry about? What there *is* to worry about is that the warmth and complexity and inexhaustibility of God's dealings with his children and of their dealings with each other are all missing.

What is true of Roman Catholics and of Protestant Fundamentalists is true of all Christian groups who are more interested in defending their own position than in following the living Spirit of God wherever it might lead. For such people, truth loses all its rough edges. The problems of theology become mere puzzles which, once the official answer is given, need no further critical examination. The mystery goes out of religion and of life; and unaccountable things, like burning bushes, lose the challenging, unexpected quality that properly belongs to them. They are passively accepted " on authority " as part of the normal furniture of existence. For all the talk that people of complacent orthodoxy make of the supernatural, the supernatural in the sense of a reality that breaks in upon human existence from the outside disappears from their lives.

The way to avoid this mystery-free dogmatism is not to try to do without clearly formulated beliefs, even though many people in the churches themselves have imagined this to be possible. The Church must have its fundamental articles of faith if it is to live, but it must be sure that it understands their real nature. The intention of the great dogmas of the Church is to remind men of the fact that they do not know what the Christian faith really is unless they see the necessity of making up their minds concerning what they believe about God's nature and the meaning of Christ and the Christian task in the world. If the Gospels make anything clear, it is that when men meet Jesus Christ they are thrust into a situation where a basic decision for or against him cannot be evaded. That decision is intimately related to what they believe him to be. Granting all that, it is still impossible to apprehend or to defend the realities that the dogmatic statements of Christian faith express, in what we call a " dogmatic " way. It is impossible to believe truly in one's heart and in the depths of one's mind that Jesus Christ is Lord simply " on authority." It is often sensible and educationally valuable to accept certain truths, even in the religious realm, " on authority " until one is in a position honestly to test them for oneself, but the basic act of faith in God is not of this order. God requires that it be an unreserved commitment of the whole person, and such commitment is impossible unless each individual faces his own difficulties for himself.

In fact, it is often implied in the Bible that a recognition that we do not have all the answers is the most appropriate attitude, and the one to which God can most readily speak. Job and the psalmists rebuke those who rush in busily to explain the will of God to their fellows and who try to act like God. " Be still, and know that I am God," says Psalm Forty-six, with the implication that the noise that men make suggests that they think that they can depose God. The way in which Jesus appealed from the surface meanings of passages in the Old Testament to their real underlying meanings, as in the Sermon on the Mount, shows that he was aware of the element of mystery in God's self-revelation, and knew how easily the " religious " could be led astray when they put their own interpretation upon that mystery. It is not an accident that the first Christian heretics were called Gnostics, people who claimed more knowledge of God than he had chosen to reveal, knowledge which merely fed their curiosity and gratified their sense of exclusive superiority without making them " wise unto salvation." The man who will believe anything, the idolator, is subject to the withering contempt of the prophets, and the man who wants crude external indications of God's presence, because he is unable to discern the true personal reality, is rebuked by Jesus as a seeker after signs.

Another way of denying the mystery is taken by people who would claim to possess a " liberal " or enlightened theological outlook, although whether theirs is the truly liberal attitude is a matter of debate. They deny the need for mystery by denying, in effect, the need for any particular revelation of God. They do not need to turn aside to see any burning bush because a burning bush is not such a remarkable object. As far as they are concerned, "every common bush" is "afire with God." They do not see the point of having the light of Christ because they do not believe that there is any deep darkness for it to illuminate. If Jesus is divine, he is divine in the sense that all men are, only more so. His divinity is absorbed into his humanity, and it fades into the light of common day.

This attitude can seem credible only to those who lead sheltered lives in places where the forces of darkness have been so successfully subdued that they hardly appear to exist. It is the attitude of "nice people," living in nice places. The modern world has provided only too many reminders that all life is not like that. It is not surprising that, despite all their advantages, the spiritual understanding of people who cherish such ideas becomes quickly trivialized. They are living only on the surface of existence.

Antireligious Denials of Mystery

Most people in these days, however, are more aware of the antireligious ways in which the mystery of life is denied, and it is certainly of great importance that these should be rightly evaluated. They take many forms but the most significant of them is that which may broadly be described by the term scientific positivism, a position held by many who may never have heard the term. In its simplest forms this view holds that life has no mysteries, only problems, problems that can be solved by the use of the scientific method, of which the best exemplification is provided by the physical sciences. Since this method cannot answer the question, Why?, the question, Why? is dismissed as irrelevant. The only question which matters is, How?

Now this attitude has been asserted with great confidence and has been widely accepted. Its chief strength lies in the fact that it can point to the dazzling achievements of the scientific method in those areas of life where it is a proper tool for investigation. A contrast can also be drawn between these positive achievements and the uncertainty and disagreements that arise whenever men move into the dimension of ultimate meanings, with which religion, the arts, and the humanities try to deal. What is more reasonable than to hold that the only solid ground we know is that of scientific knowledge, and that other realms are either best ignored or treated as interesting diversions? Such an attitude gives people an excuse for averting their eyes from the bewildering complexity of their real situation as human beings. It also becomes more attractive when it ministers to the scientist's already considerable sense of his own importance in the scheme of things. As W. H. Auden has said, betraying his English background, "When I am in the company of scientists in these days, I feel like a curate in a roomful of dukes."

It needs to be asserted, in the most direct way, that to hold that life's problems are all that deserve our attention, and that its mystery can be ignored, is arbitrary and unproved. What is more, such an attitude flies in the face of the most fundamental human experience and contradicts the way in which defenders of the position actually behave. It has often been pointed out that the scientist, who insists that the only real knowledge is that which is scientifically measurable, will be as eager as the next man to know whether the girl he loves is prepared to marry him, or even whether the results of his experiments are likely to enhance his professional reputation. To say that the personal dimension, which is that of mystery, is irrelevant is simply to try to withdraw from the distinctively human situation and to try to wish into being a world other than the one in which we all actually live.

It is an ironic comment on the confusion and failure of

spiritual insight in our time that this frivolous and superficial attitude should have acquired an air of unusual realism and practicality. Yet it is similar to the idolatry which the Bible condemns, and it is very different from the genuine wonder and questioning of the true scientific attitude, which is not far from the Biblical attitude of wonder in the presence of all creation. The fundamental objection to all such philosophies is that they provide no reason why anything should exist rather than nothing. They miss the mystery of existence, out of whose apprehension philosophy and science are born. Their philosophy is the denial of philosophy.

The rest of us are entitled to insist, therefore, that the fact that some people ignore the basic life questions is no reason why we should do the same. Is it really possible to live without trying to find out why we should suffer and toil and sacrifice and enjoy? What is the status of the almost universal belief that there are such things as truth and error, and that goodness and beauty are preferable to evil and ugliness? Why are we like what we are, brought into existence with such apparent fortuitousness, insignificant specks on a tiny planet in the midst of a gigantic universe that is marvelously adapted to our needs and bursts with vitality and meaning? Or, as we so frequently remind ourselves, why are we able to grasp with our minds the immensities of the universe in which we live and, what is much more important, to subdue it increasingly to our purposes? And why, although we seem to be the products of a long process of natural selection broadly continuous with that of the nonhuman creation around us, do we possess not merely consciousness but also conscience? Above all, why, as creatures of a brief season, do we long for eternity and give overwhelming priority to our relations, not with the world around us, but with each other, believing that in these we come closer to enduring reality than in any other way?

These, of course, are the familiar, age-old questions that lie behind the whole history of human reflection and aspiration. There is no need to discuss them further at this stage. But it is worth laboring the point that we have a right to ask them because, in a confused time like the present, our hesitancy about their status has inhibited many people from asking them as frankly as they might and from taking enough time and trouble to discover adequate answers.

It is, perhaps, chiefly in this sense that it can be said that the rise of modern science has made it more difficult for men to believe in the Christian God. We are, it is true, more conscious than our fathers were of the difference between the outlook on life of men influenced by the scientific method and that of the men of the Bible. This creates difficult problems. But those problems are not insoluble, and there are many Christian writers, professional scientists and others, who show us ways in which they can be solved. It is very misleading to suppose that the men of the Bible found it easy to believe in God, or that the fundamental objections to that belief are those which arise because of the discoveries of modern science, or that there is anything new about them. These objections arise out of the human situation as such. The damage done by the rise of modern science has been indirect, and has been more obvious among the general public than among outstanding scientists. It has made people lose their confidence in the status of the personal dimension of experience and to distrust the authority of theologians and artists and philosophers who have devoted most attention to that dimension.

The consequences of this loss of confidence have been very serious and it is essential that they should be honestly faced if we are to have a right attitude today toward the question of belief in God. So far are the people of this generation from being more enlightened and skeptical than their forefathers were that the opposite is probably true. The question of belief in God arises primarily in the personal, or as it is sometimes called the subjective, dimension of experience. This dimension has not received the attention it deserves in modern times. Our concentration on science and even more on technology and commerce has led us, not to ignore the personal dimension because that is impossible, but to shrink from making the disciplined efforts to reach understanding that are necessary in this field. Our approach to matters of religion and the arts, and such distinctively human affairs as politics, as well as to entertainment, has been that of the " tired businessman." This is not surprising because business has been the main interest of our life. The modern world has had to pay a very heavy price for its rapid material advance. In the long perspective of history, that price may have proved to be worth paying, but only if its heaviness is clearly recognized and we realize how hard we have to work in order to rebuild our spiritual capital.

It is important to note that a strong reaction against this mood of scientific positivism is under way and gathering momentum at present. Technological institutions insist on the importance of a general education in liberal arts and some of the larger and more enlightened corporations strongly encourage this insistence. And the atomic scientists, faced with the startling human implications of their discoveries, have seen with peculiar clarity, sometimes even more clearly than the preachers, that human problems can be solved only in a human way. This may be comforting on one level but it does not alter the fact that the pervasive influence of scientific positivism, which has fostered an attitude of indifference and distrust toward the dimension of mystery, remains strong and will continue to keep us ignorant and confused for a long time to come.

The need must be emphasized, therefore, for a certain humility and hesitancy and expectancy in approaching the question of belief in God. Ecclesiastical self-righteousness assumes too readily that it knows all the answers. Quasi-scientific self-righteousness discourages us from taking the trouble to formulate the questions properly. The mystery of existence seems to escape the ken of both. Yet the question of belief in God is the greatest and most far-reaching of human questions. It is essential that our spirits should be fully extended in approaching it and that we should feel free to call upon all the resources that are available in trying to answer it.

2

CAN WE PROVE THAT GOD EXISTS?

The Traditional Proofs of God's Existence

The customary approach to discussions of belief in God, at least in the textbooks, has been by examining proofs for his existence. The history of thought is full of attempts to show that God's existence can be proved by the unaided reason reflecting on the nature of the world and of human experience, without reference to any of the data provided by Christian or any other kind of special revelation. These efforts go back ultimately to the Greeks, but they reached their climax in the Church, particularly in the Western Church of the Middle Ages.

These proofs have been discussed and restated, attacked and defended, right up to our own day. The best-known of them are, to give them their ponderous academic names, the cosmological, teleological, and ontological. Alongside them is a much more modern proof, which is on a different level, the moral argument for the existence of God. We shall not examine these proofs in detail but try to give a brief indication of their value and limitations. It will be convenient to leave discussion of the ontological proof till a later part of this chapter.

The *cosmological* argument is a rather technical argument from the necessity of a first cause. Everything we know is caused by something else, but there cannot be an infinite regress; there must be a "first cause." Implied in the causal system, therefore, is a primary cause, which necessarily contains the causal system as its effect. This primary cause is God.

The *teleological* argument, or the argument from design, is not unlike the cosmological but it is less technical in form and it has always been the argument with the greatest appeal for ordinary people. No one can deny that there is the most remarkable correspondence between our minds and the structure of the universe around them, a correspondence which makes the researches of the scientist himself possible. The primary cause of the universe must have some rational character, which gives it its kinship with human reason. The more modern science discovers of the universe, the more this seems to be borne out, with ever-increasing richness and detail. And there is not only order: there is beauty. Is it conceivable that a lovely countryside, bursting with new life in springtime, or the human body in its full glory, are the products of a fortuitous collocation of powers, which know no law other than the blind urge of their own internal development? The argument becomes even stronger when it is related to human creativity. Man's ability to create meaningful and purposive forms, whether through co-operative enterprises like the building of great corporations and universities, or through individual achievements like composing symphonies, provides striking examples of the fact that there does appear to be purpose running through life.

Of course there is another side to the story, as the opponents of the teleological argument have been quick to point out. Disorder, ugliness, death, and a host of other apparently pointless things exist. These certainly cannot be ignored and we shall be considering them in another context in the fifth chapter. They undoubtedly suffice to deny any clinching validity to the argument from design when it stands by itself, and make inappropriate the complacency with which some people have used it. The Christian who understands the real grounds of his assurance will not merely be prepared to admit this but be anxious to insist upon it.

Yet there is this to be said about the considerations to which these two " proofs " call attention. They may be inconclusive, but ordinary experience inevitably finds itself giving them a good deal of weight when it ponders upon the meaning of life. Let it be agreed that it is possible that the world may be a self-generating machine or, as the philosopher David Hume implied, a vast self-creating organism, and that all its infinitely detailed order and splendor, so wonderfully attuned to our hearts and minds, are its accidental by-products. It is possible, but is it likely? If it requires the eye of faith to see that " the heavens are telling the glory of God; and the firmament proclaims his handiwork," it requires an eye darkened either by sin or folly to refuse to see that there is glory in the heavens and that the firmament is the handiwork of a creative power.

This may be one of the places where the self-confidence of scientific positivism has made the observant person lose confidence in his own most authentic insights. That the evidence of the teleological argument is inconclusive does not mean that it has no weight at all. The evidence continues to demand an explanation, even if that provided by the argument itself cannot carry full conviction. More than that, it can be said that the probabilities are in favor of the view that the purpose, order, and beauty of the world express the purpose, order, and beauty of a Being, not ourselves, who made them, rather than of a view that says that they have no discoverable significance.

Considerations of this kind gain even more weight when the *moral* argument is examined. When this argument received its classic formulation by the German philosopher Kant, it was held to mark a great step forward. It shifted the discussion from that of the nature of the external world to that of man himself, and his self-consciousness. It registered the conviction that the meaning of human life was to be found primarily within the personal dimension of experience. Two things seemed to be self-evidently real to Kant, the starry heavens above and the moral law within, by which he meant that there are certain things that we know we " ought " to do. Of these the latter was the more important, and from consideration of its nature he derived his three great postulates, God, freedom, and immortality. The moral law was such that it demanded the reality of God. Many philosophers have followed a similar road since Kant. Their faith has been, in the words of a title of a famous book by A. E. Taylor, *The Faith of a Moralist.*

In justifying this faith, they have had to face many objections, some of the most forcible from the theological side itself. The question has been raised whether the moral law is quite so self-evidently authoritative as Kant and his successors have made it out to be. Psychological study has shown how we are all influenced by deep-rooted instincts and urges even in our formulation of the moral law. Anthropology has shown how relative most men's interpretations of it are. Besides, modern men have become much more aware of the ease with which individuals and groups can find good reasons to justify their own established customs or even their self-interest. Can the moral argument be stated in a way which avoids these dangers? Many thinkers in the nineteenth century, and many ordinary people in the twentieth, have become conscious of the threat of ultimate meaninglessness, which finds expression in the philosophical attitude called nihilism. Their difficulty is precisely their inability to accept the self-evident authority of the moral law within. The question has to be asked whether the moral law itself does not stand in need of justification by a self-disclosure of God as the source of goodness and righteousness rather than the other way round.

We have already suggested, however, that what was true in the case of the other arguments is even more obviously true here. Formidable as the objections may be to the moral argument as a proof of God's existence, the facts of the moral life remain and require to be accounted for. Men everywhere have a sense of right and wrong, and the more successful as human beings they become, the more delicate, intense, far-reaching and compelling that sense of right and wrong is. There is a certain speciousness about all attempts to read it out of human experience. Its expression may vary widely from one individual or culture to another but that does not alter the fact that it is always present and seems to be bound up with human nature as such. Even the most depraved evildoer pays his inverted testimony to its reality, if only by trying to prove that he is not really as evil as men make out. In so far as he is genuinely amoral, he is regarded as less than a typical human being. If it be granted that there are dark corners and depths in experience that most formulations of the moral argument do not adequately take into account, does that alter the fact that the moral life, so far as it goes, seems to be the response, whether in co-operation or resistance, to " a power not ourselves which makes for righteousness "? Once more, whatever men may say with the tops of their minds, most of them behave as though this were their real belief.

All these attempts to prove God's existence must, therefore, be taken as inconclusive but not necessarily as insignificant just because they are inconclusive. They call attention to aspects of universal human experience that demand explanation and are a standing challenge to those who dogmatically assert that there is no God. That it is at least as difficult to dispose of them as it is to accept them shows that they have real value in keeping the discussion open. They point us to the mysterious character of life and the need to discover ultimate meanings. But to lay too much stress upon them and, in particular, to regard them as the source of a stronger assurance of God's reality than his self-disclosure in Christ, is dangerously misleading.

Revelation and Reason

Too much emphasis on the traditional proofs for God's existence is misleading for three reasons. First, if we insist that they furnish proofs rather than pointers, we are led to think of God in ways very different from those in which Christians have been led to think of him. The God reached by way of the traditional proofs becomes so cold and featureless that men cannot easily live with him and they are led to project their own ideas, and sometimes their own prejudices, into their notion of him. He is a God derived from the world, who is caught within the world. As such, this God of the philosophers is much more open to the charge of being a wish fulfillment than the God of the Bible.

Secondly, it has often been noticed that if you look at the history of these proofs, it becomes clear that they have usually proved acceptable only to those who have been disposed to believe in God on other grounds. The attitude of medieval thinkers was that of people looking for confirmation of something that they already knew to be true. The moral argument was clutched at eagerly by Protestants in the nineteenth century because they were looking for a justification of their continuing belief that God was real, personal, just, and loving, at a time when they were dubious of the power of the Christian faith alone to authenticate itself as true. What these proofs try to do, in effect, is to give a rational justification for an act of faith that is made on a deeper level than that of argument alone.

The chief interest of the *ontological* proof, or the proof from the nature of the divine being, lies in its partial recognition of this fact. When this is realized, it helps us to understand the curious part that this proof has played in the history of thought. It was first formulated by Anselm, Archbishop of Canterbury, in the twelfth century. He said that the idea of God could be defined as that than which nothing greater can be conceived. But, he argued, if that is so, God's existence must be included in the very idea, because, if he did not exist, a being with the further perfection of existence would be greater than he, and hence God.

This argument has created a great deal of bewilderment. People have protested that all this seems too simple, echoing Kant's famous observation that to have the idea of one hundred dollars is not the same as having them in one's pocket. At the same time, they have felt that there is more in this than can be dismissed with a smart contradiction. The difficulty is partly overcome when it is remembered that the argument did not arise as a general piece of philosophizing. It arose in the context of a prayer for illumination which Anselm offered when his faith had been attacked. The objection that his opponent had made was that God was no more than a figment of the imagination.

This difficulty drives Anselm almost to despair, but he then receives the insight that makes him say that God is that than which nothing greater can be conceived. He sees that if the atheist retorts that this is still his own imagination, Anselm can reply that clearly the atheist is not talking about the same reality as he is. Once the atheist thinks of the idea of God as one produced by himself, he is not thinking about God.

Anselm is, in fact, trying to explain the character of reality that the act of faith possesses. He is convinced and immensely encouraged by his discovery of this argument because he already knows what God is like, as he has known him in Jesus

Christ. Anselm is not a detached observer of the human situation, who has lighted upon the hypothesis of God as the most likely explanation of the meaning of existence; he is the man of faith finding convincing intellectual expression of what has come to him in revelation.

The third objection to taking the traditional proofs as sufficient grounds for belief in God is the most serious of all. It is that life does not really pose the question of belief in the way in which the proofs do. The picture that we often like to draw of ourselves, as detached intelligences rigorously scrutinizing the evidence to see whether it points to the reality of God or not, is far from the truth. For this question is not like a mathematical problem that can be solved without affecting our personal lives. Nor is it simply an interesting point of speculation, which can arouse curiosity if presented attractively enough in a bull session, but which can be taken up or dropped according to mood, like discussions of the occult or of the meaning of dreams. The question of God's existence cannot be answered on one level of experience alone. It plunges us into the realm of ultimate meanings. It makes us ask ourselves whether we are living as we should, and it challenges our self-esteem. Our deepest hopes and fears are involved, and we quickly find ourselves fighting for our lives.

Let us remind ourselves again that these considerations do not mean that the question can only be answered in an irrational manner or with a great show of emotion. On the contrary, our minds should never be more fully alert than here. What is meant is that we should not deceive ourselves that we are proceeding rationally when we are not, and that we should realize the full difficulties of trying to think rationally about God.

Religion is a most embarrassing subject. Nowhere is it more difficult for men to be honest than when they are approaching religion. Nothing is easier than to imagine that one is seeking the objective truth, when all that one is doing is either seeking ready confirmation of a faith one is too timid or lazy to scrutinize, or looking for a justification to continue in uncritical disbelief. To imagine that our own reasons are the only reliable courts of appeal in trying to discover grounds for belief in God, covers up the fundamental difficulty, which is that we are not disinterested persons in this matter.

Of course, the word " reason," like the word " faith," can be used in several different senses, and this is a frequent source of confusion. It is important for our present purpose to distinguish two senses, heavy as the going may initially seem in doing so. The *first* is reason in the sense of " reasoning," the ability to put two and two together and generally figure things out. This is one of the most necessary and noblest of human abilities. Any religion that depreciates it or sets it aside is by that act branded as a superstition. There can be no conflict between faith and reason in this sense, provided that faith is genuine and that reason is functioning properly, because faith must commend itself to and find its fulfillment in this reason before it can be fully appropriated. Faith must make sense, because we are constitutionally incapable of believing real nonsense. To be sure, there are difficulties. The relation between the truth that faith presents to the rational faculty, and the truth that scientific knowledge presents, is sometimes hard to see. But these difficulties must be worked through by rational means to a rational conclusion.

It is when reason is thought of in a *second* sense that the familiar conflict between faith and reason emerges. Reason is here thought of much more actively, as the means by which we are aware of ourselves and relate ourselves to the general meaning of life. It is reason as used in stating our deepest convictions. This is more characteristically associated with preachers or artists or classical philosophers than with scientists or technicians. Complications arise because we often think that we are using reason in the first sense when we are actually using it in this second sense. We are tempted to do this because we like to claim the prestige of the objectivity of reason in the first sense for our own convictions.

One of the assertions of the Christian faith is that man is sinful, that he possesses a spirit within him that resents God's right to be God and that tries to force him out of his proper place. The root of this rebellion may be more readily found in the will than in the reason, but it spreads into the reason also. Indeed, to the extent to which this reason is cherished and cultivated, this rebellion becomes all the more visible in it. Just as a state will use its propaganda organization to justify its actions in a war, so the proud spirit of man tries to justify to itself its rebellion against God, looking always for good reasons why it should ignore or defy God.

When faith comes, it must inevitably seem to be the contradiction of this kind of reason. As Paul says, it is foolishness to them that are perishing. When a man commits himself in faith to Christ, however, and looks out on life as one whose eyes have been opened by Christ, his deepest and most sincere conviction is that he has had a right reason restored to him. He is able to see things as they really are, without a false image of himself getting in the way. He is in a right relation to God, the source of all truth, whose very foolishness is wiser than the best wisdom of rebellious men.

What makes this situation puzzling to the unbeliever and difficult for the believer is that the truth of this analysis of the relation between faith and reason becomes visible only to the person who has known the experience of faith. Christians should know from their own experience that God has his own ways of commending his truth even to the rebellious reason of man, and his dealings are so personal that the story of how he does this varies from one individual to another. What is important is that, in their natural anxiety to persuade their neighbors of the truth of the Christian faith, Christians should not weaken the force of the Christian challenge to the rebellious reason of man by assuming that there is some safe neutral ground between faith and unbelief where both can walk together. On the contrary, the more fundamental the knowledge with which we are dealing, the more clearly will our attitude toward it be determined by our attitude toward belief in God.

The rationality of faith can best be served, therefore, not by trying to show the unbeliever how reasonable it is from the point of view of his own man-centered outlook but by compelling him to review his criterion of what constitutes rational knowledge. Faith begins its work by compelling a man to look at himself with fresh eyes and ask himself whether he is as honest as he likes to think he is. It presents him with new facts and compels him to look at familiar facts in a new light. In all this, it presupposes the sound working of his reasoning instrument, of reason in our first sense, and it rebukes as an evasion of its own challenge any attempt to take refuge in a blind irrationality. The aim of faith is to help a man come to himself, like the prodigal, by receiving the mind of Christ, the truly reasonable Man.

The Difficulty of Honesty

Three other closely connected considerations are worth bearing in mind in approaching belief in God.

The first is that we cannot take the purity of our motives for granted. There is nothing on which self-consciously modern people pride themselves more than their sincerity and their integrity. Yet mature psychological study in our own day has made clear the extent to which our thinking is motivated, not by what we consciously assert, but by deep urges of pride and timidity, and by desires for security and conformity. This fact has often been used to confound the pretensions of religious people, sometimes with considerable justice. But those who have been quickest to point out these things in relation to the religious, have not always seen that the same influences may be at work in their own attitude. One of the most revealing examples of this attitude at work occurs in an article written by George Bernard Shaw shortly before his death. He was reviewing the biography of Samuel Butler, the author of *The Way of All Flesh,* one of the classic accounts of Victorian loss of faith. Shaw confessed that much of the enthusiasm with which the intellectuals of the nineteenth century took up the cause of evolution was not because they had soberly reached the conclusion that it was true, but because it provided them with a good stick with which to beat the clergy, whom they disliked for a variety of personal reasons.

Similarly, it is easy to imagine that one is seriously inquiring whether one believes in God, when all that one is doing is trying to find reasons to buttress an already existing uncritical faith, or, on the other hand, trying to find an excuse for disposing of the whole matter as not worthy of attention. Pastors are familiar with how often people make up their minds about the Christian faith on grounds which are quite irrelevant to the issue. It is easy to laugh at the lady who loses her faith because the minister's wife forgot to invite her to the tea party, but the reasons that others give are not always radically different in kind. People try to analyze their attitude to the truths of Christian faith and they are immediately distracted by the image of their beloved mother, from whom they first heard those truths, and they look at them through the emotional haze induced by that memory. Or, on the other side, they im-

mediately think of a particularly boring and pompous clergyman who afflicted their childhood and imagine they are making
up their minds about God when they are really making up
their minds about that clergyman. Of course, the testimony of
the mother and the clergyman are not in themselves entirely
irrelevant. That is part of the difficulty. But we can seriously
mislead ourselves unless we realize that they often complicate
the question more than they should and fail to make us see, for
example, that God may not exist because of our mother, or that
he may exist despite the clergyman.

The familiarity of the Christian faith is a second obstacle to
those brought up in churchgoing communities in the Western
world. It is so much a part of the background of our minds
that we do not realize its distinctive quality or envisage what
a world would be like where life was lived on the assumption
that it and the values it taught men to cherish were not seriously regarded. One of the virtues of travel to parts of the
world where Christianity has had little influence is that it
makes it possible for us to see this more clearly. Furthermore,
the very fact that Christianity has become so well-established
and pervasive in the Western world means that its influence is
often diluted and corrupted and that many of the institutions
that express it are old and tired. Much of the objection to
Christianity that people express today is, in fact, an expression
of repugnance toward a worn-out ecclesiastical tradition that
courts popularity at too high a price. It is necessary and worth-
while to make an effort to capture that freshness of vision
which those Gentiles must have had in the ancient world when
Paul first came among them preaching the resurrection, if we
are to make a responsible decision for or against God in Christ.

The third point is closely associated with the above. It is essential that the Christian message about God should be examined in terms of what it claims to be. This fact should be

obvious but it often is not. Many people today, especially in Western countries, are prepared to acknowledge that " religion is a good thing." The way in which they say this, however, often implies that they think that all religions are very much alike and, therefore, that the claims of the particular religions are not to be taken too seriously. Their God is not the King of all the earth, with whom all men have in the last resort to deal. He is the private deity of those who are interested in religion and, if anyone does not happen to be the kind of person who is interested in religion, he does not suffer any greater deprivation than he would if he had no ear for music or no taste for poetry. However, to imagine that one is making up one's mind about the *Christian* faith when one is thinking in these terms is to be grossly deceived.

Christ claims to be the truth, and the God in whose name he speaks claims to be the God of all men, the Maker and sustainer of all life, to whom all have to render their account. What he requires of men is that they decide where they stand in relation to that claim. And men cannot do so without being altogether involved. " Behold," says the psalmist, " thou desirest truth in the inward being," and it is a sincere and unreserved commitment to its full permanent reality that the Christian faith requires of us. To patronize it as a benevolent system of semi-illusory ideas suitable to various temperaments, or as a seemly form of expressing reverence for our ancestors, is to make a mockery of the living God. As we turn to deal with the distinctive Christian belief about God let us be clear, at least, that this is the kind of claim that has to be faced.

GOD IN JESUS CHRIST

Why Turn to the Bible?

Why do we go specifically to the Bible to discover reasons for belief in God? If it be granted that the rational proofs raise questions rather than answer them and that the answers must be looked for in the religious dimension, why turn so narrowly to the religion of the Jews and to the Christian faith that arose out of it? It is certainly true that the story of religion is very much greater than that of the Bible and of the Christian Church, and that its significance for understanding the human situation is immense. When the vast number of those who hold devoted allegiance to Buddhism or Hinduism or Islam is remembered and when the great traditions of teaching and devotion of these faiths are recalled, it is impossible to deny that they must play some great part in the purpose of God. If we do not here go into the question of what that part might be, it is for these reasons.

First, these other religions are extremely hard to understand. The world of experience in which they move is so different from that of the Christian West that it is not easy for anyone to grasp what they teach unless he is in close touch with the life of these religions. This is the mistake made by those people who naïvely advocate that children in schools should be taught all the chief religions of the world, as well as the Christian, so that they can be free to make up their minds which is the best to follow. Children should certainly be taught something about other religions, but it is frivolous to suggest that they can capture much of their spirit and therefore make a responsible decision about them in the atmosphere of a Western school. How can we be sure that it is Hinduism or Buddhism or Mohammedanism that is actually conveyed, when the religion in question is taught by someone whose knowledge of it is based on a textbook written by a Christian missionary or a Western intellectual, and learned by children who bring all kinds of unexamined assumptions from a radically different world to its study? To convey Christianity is hard enough; to convey other religions even with a minimal accuracy is almost impossible.

The questions of the status of other religions, and the related matter of whether there is a distinctive essence of religion common to all faiths are important questions, but they must be the themes of other books than this. It is essential to realize that other religions exist, and there can be little doubt that the careful study of them will throw important light on our understanding of the Christian faith. One challenge they present will be unavoidable in our last chapter. But it is quite unrealistic to pretend that their main challenge can be met by any except those who are directly confronted by them, and Islam and Buddhism are not really live options in Texas and Maine. Those Christians who meet such a challenge assure us that, while other religions raise great questions and throw new light on many aspects of Christian faith, they do not lend encouragement to the belief that they and Christian faith can be subsumed in an underlying unity of all religions, or that such other religions provide more faithful knowledge of the living God than Christ does. It is, therefore, to the revelation of which the

Bible speaks that we turn. A further discussion of the relationship of Christianity to other religions will be found in another volume in this series, *A Faith for the Nations,* by Charles Forman.

Christians turn to the Bible because they believe that it is the record of the self-disclosure of God in a special way, reaching its fulfillment in the unique person of Jesus Christ. That fact is well-known but it is not always seen in the proper context. It is wrong to think of Jesus simply as an isolated figure who compels attention by the quality of his personal influence and who so inspires our confidence that, when he speaks of his Heavenly Father, he makes us believe in him too. Jesus is often presented in that way today, but that is not the only or the chief way in which the Gospels reveal him. They present him as the crown and climax of a long historical movement and, unless he is clearly seen in the setting of that movement, the meaning of the Biblical revelation of God cannot be properly grasped.

It was emphasized at the outset that the Bible laid stress on the mystery of life. In the preceding chapter we also saw that it was important to look at the Christian faith with fresh eyes. The Bible has become so much a part of the furniture of existence, even if it is not read very much, that it is easy to take for granted what it says and to assume that we know what it means. Yet, in fact, it contains the most strange and remarkable story in human history.

The Uniqueness of the Bible

This strange and remarkable quality is partly concealed by the fact that the Bible appears to start with a rational account of the creation of the world and man, together with a story about the origin of sin, which may predispose us to believe that it is claiming to be a history of all mankind, and one of dubious accuracy. It is one of the many benefits of modern critical study of the Biblical text that we are enabled to see that something rather different is involved. Those wonderful opening stories in Genesis are of immense spiritual value, but all the evidence goes to show that they were written, and then rewritten, at comparatively late stages in the history of Israel, after men had had time to reflect profoundly on the meaning of the dealings with them of a God they had already experienced.

If the account in Genesis is studied carefully against its background, it becomes clear that the first sign of God's *historical* activity which we have recorded for us is the call of Abraham. Consider the strangeness and wonder that surround this event. From the frontiers of human memory there comes this story of a man, like other men, who is brought face to face with Another. Whoever Abraham may have been, and whether he was a particular individual or the focus of the folk memory, the fact remains that the Other made clear-cut demands on him in such a way as to call forth his obedience. It is also clear that the Other made a promise that if Abraham committed himself into His hands, He would make his descendants to be a great and mighty people.

The same sense of a mysterious purpose, which men can neither define nor evade, broods over the rest of the stories of the patriarchs. There is Jacob wrestling with the mysterious stranger who will not reveal his name, and suddenly realizing that a particular place is charged with a more than human presence; there is Joseph, seeing that a story of family treachery and reconciliation is part of a wider purpose. All these familiar stories we learned at Sunday school, without always knowing what they implied, say more to us than we once thought.

Suddenly, things break out from this remote world into one

more like that of history as we know it. The descendants of
Joseph are virtual slaves in Egypt, where they appear to have
settled after Joseph, and the promise to Abraham seems to have
been forgotten. But a mysterious power breaks into their lives
again. A young man of curious ancestry is guarding some flocks
when, according to the story, he sees a bush that burns, yet is
not consumed by its fire. This inspired symbol of the living,
inexhaustible God, which has always captured the Christian
imagination, is a sign that calls the young man's attention to
the presence of One who is other and greater than himself, and
who has a purpose for his people Israel. Moses is to deliver
them from Egypt and lead them to a promised land of their
own. There follows the story of the Exodus from Egypt.

The importance of the Exodus for Israel can hardly be
exaggerated. It imprinted indelibly on the mind of the nation
the conviction that they were a people called to dwell in a
special relation with their God. We cannot be certain that all
the events described in connection with the Exodus, the
plagues, the smiting of the first born, and the crossing of the
Red Sea, took place precisely as described, but one thing is
clear. An event which deserves the title of " miraculous " undoubtedly took place. A group of slaves who were, as their
descendants described them, " no people," part of the disin-
herited masses of mankind, are somehow transformed into a
people who have enough faith in God to allow themselves to
be led to a land that they believe he has prepared for them.
That this was no mere dramatized folk myth of the national
origins is shown, not merely by the realistic psychological insight of the narrative, which in no way idealizes the Israelites,
but also by the great experience that followed on from the
Exodus, the giving of the law on Sinai. In a setting of the ut-
most solemnity and majesty, they are made to see that the ad-
venture upon which they have embarked involves them in the

effort to become a different kind of people, with a new and
nobler pattern of existence. The Ten Commandments are the
ethical implication of the deliverance from Egypt. The Exodus
made a profound change in the whole attitude of Israel. The
covenant (or "agreement") that God had made with them
had indeed made them a nation set apart, a holy nation. The
hand of the living God was here at work.

The rest of the Old Testament is dominated by these events.
The people finally settle in the Promised Land. They appoint
a king and, with some misgivings, they make a permanent
abode in the Temple at Jerusalem for the most sacred symbol
of God's presence in their midst, the Ark of the Covenant.
After this, there develops a long debate between God and
Israel, the Lord's controversy with his people. The Israelites
behave in the typical human way. They have the Exodus behind them and they live in the Promised Land, yet they chafe
under the burden of obedience to their God. It is not so much
that they call into question God's reality and his purpose but
that they live as though God did not matter much. They want
God, but they want him on their own terms. The covenant
ceases to impose an unlimited commitment upon them, or so
they believe. They assume that their part of it can be fulfilled
by sacrifices and rituals. And they begin to take worldly pride
in being Israelites and boast of their privileges among the
nations.

In this situation men arise who make clear that Israel is
denying her vocation. They are the prophets, who claim to
speak under the constraint of God's truth, and who remind the
people of the real nature of their God and of his covenant.
These reminders are given, not as abstract pieces of teaching,
but in specific relation to the lives of the people, to social injustices, to the threat of invasion, to exile and the return from
exile. A new self-consciousness is born in Israel as a result of

her failure to keep the covenant. The great prophets come to see that if the Lord's promise is to be fulfilled, it must be through a new kind of servant of the Lord, who will not only open up the way for the fulfillment of Israel's destiny but also make up for the failure of Israel through his own self-sacrifice. And as men ponder upon God's nature and action, they see that he is not merely the private God of Israel but the Lord of heaven and earth and that all men must find their ultimate destiny in him.

Jesus Christ and Belief in God

It is against this background that Jesus Christ appears. This it not the place to attempt a full account of the work and person of Jesus Christ (further discussion of the person and work of Christ will be found in another volume in this series, *The Meaning of Christ,* by Robert Johnson), but it must be realized that the evidence provided by Jesus is of the first importance in answering the question of God's reality. It is sometimes assumed that what we make of the impact of Jesus depends on the attitude toward God's existence that we bring to it, an attitude reached on other grounds. The truth is that the impact of Jesus itself provides essential evidence in helping us decide whether we believe in God.

The timing of the coming of Jesus Christ partakes to the full of the strangeness and mystery of human existence. Paul says that " when the time had fully come, God sent forth his Son," that is, when the time was ripe, but it is not really very obvious why he should have come at that time rather than another. He appears, heralded by the enigmatic figure of John the Baptist and by the religious movements connected with him.

Whatever else may be true of Jesus, it is clear that he was

human, a man among men. That means that the questions of God's reality and the nature of his own vocation as a representative of Israel were posed for Jesus in the same way as they are for any other man. It is true, of course, that he does not appear to have indulged in generalized philosophical discussions about the existence and nature of God, any more than any other of the great figures of the Bible did. But his deep and agonizing inquiries into God's purpose were all the more searching because they were the Jewish way of raising the question of truth, truth which affected action. A superficial reading of the wonderful story of the temptations may suggest that the temptations are rejections of inadequate ways of fulfilling God's purpose. But this is only superficial. The temptations are desperate onslaughts of unbelief. The evil one denies God's right to be God, and that is the essence of unbelief. The same is true in a different way of the agony in Gethsemane. And as Jesus hangs upon the cross, the challenge of unbelief to the reality of God receives its ultimate expression in the mocking cry, " If you are the Son of God, come down from the cross."

It is essential that we see how the whole question concerning the reality of the Christian God gathers to a head in the cross and resurrection of Christ. Unless we do, the reality of God becomes a matter of interesting speculation rather than one that genuinely determines human destiny. Nowhere is the reality of God and the covenant he made with Israel put to the test more searchingly than in these tremendous events. All the threats to meaning in human life are gathered up in the expiring cry of Jesus as he hangs upon the cross, " My God, my God, why hast thou forsaken me? " And all the hopes of the fulfillment of true life in eternity go with his lifeless body into the tomb. If Jesus lived and died in vain, the Christian God does not exist.

It was out of the conviction that God in Jesus Christ had proved himself stronger than the cross and the tomb, that the Christian faith was born. The evidence for this conviction is given in the resurrection experience, which was the supreme vindication of the faith of Jesus. That is why Easter has always been recognized as the most distinctive festival of the Church's life and why, in its periods of clear vision, the Church has always insisted that belief in the Christian God depends on knowledge of the risen Christ.

The resurrection story, as it is told in the Gospels, confronts our minds with many difficulties. It is true that in the Gospel narratives there are many discrepancies and difficulties, and it is hard to know just what the " facts " are. If what we are asked to believe is simply that a man who was dead appeared alive on earth for a brief period, we are right to protest that the evidence is inadequate. We have it only from the lips of his own followers that it was so, and it is told in a curiously excited, inconsequential way. If sworn affidavits were available from Caiaphas and Pontius Pilate and an independent committee of observers from outside Jerusalem, we should be the more disposed to believe such an unlikely story.

But this is not what we are asked to believe. We are asked to believe that a power, which men have experienced as an active, living reality from that day to this, proved itself stronger than the shock of death and the concentrated impact of evil, and that the sign of this victory was the resurrection appearance of Christ.

If we read the Gospels carefully, we see that the apostles are not really interested in " proving " that Jesus had appeared alive. The reason for this is clear to anyone who has any understanding of what authentic Christian experience is like. The Gospels were written for believers, " through faith for faith," that is to say, *by* those who knew the active power of Christ in their lives and *for* those whose closest bond with them was that they knew the same power. The first readers of the Gospels did not need to have the resurrection of Christ proved to them because their faith itself carried with it the assurance that it had happened. What the Gospel writers provide is more detail than their readers possessed about the event itself and more insight into its meaning.

It is inevitable, therefore, that the stories of the resurrection, if they are considered by themselves, should raise difficulties for modern minds. They are credible only as part of the full experience of God in Christ. But it is essential that their difficulty should not be used as a reason for evading their challenge and for trying to make an acceptable version of Christianity without them. For it is only when the meaning of the cross and resurrection is honestly faced that the most urgent difficulties that confront the Christian believers are met and overcome. As P. T. Forsyth, the great British theologian of the last generation, said, " The result of his life and teaching was that they all forsook him and fled; but the result of his cross, resurrection, and glory was to rally them and to create the Church in which he dwells."

The reason why " his cross, resurrection, and glory " created the Church is that not until the cross and resurrection did it become decisively clear that the power that was in Christ was stronger than the powers of sin and evil and death. These had done their worst when men had nailed him to the cross, yet he triumphed over them and returned, bearing his human body with him, to the God from whom he had come. When his disciples were gathered together in one place on the Day of Pentecost, still overwhelmed and confused by the impact of these great events, they had a further experience. (See Acts, ch. 2.) This drove home to them the two facts on which the future of their community, which came to be known as the

Church of Jesus Christ, was based.

The first was that although Jesus Christ had left them, the power that was in him was freely available for them also. As he had promised, he had indeed not left them comfortless but had sent them his Holy Spirit, to unite and guide and sustain them in the fulfillment of his will.

The second fact was that the source of the power that had been in Christ and that they knew in the Spirit was none other than the God of Israel and the King of all the earth. Christ did more than define the nature of God more clearly and vividly than ever before. After all, the prophets of Israel had done a great deal in that direction, and he followed quite consciously in their succession. He had also vindicated the power of God in action and by overcoming the barrier of their sins had made God's reconciling power available to all men. He had made a new covenant (or agreement) between God and man, which fulfilled and transcended the covenant made with Abraham, and henceforward no man could truly come to the Father except by him.

It was because of the character of this experience of God in his revelation that the Church was led to speak of him as a Trinity, Father, Son, and Holy Spirit. This was not done as a kind of game in celestial mathematics, although it might sometimes seem like that to anyone unfamiliar with the realities with which the early Christians were dealing. The Church arose out of the old Israel, which believed passionately in the unity and sovereignty of God. Nevertheless, it was driven to formulate the doctrine of the Trinity as an act of obedience to that very God because, in the exercise of his Lordship, he had chosen to make himself known in three ways, as Father, Son, and Holy Spirit, and yet in doing so to remain recognizably and indivisibly as himself.

It is true that the New Testament itself does not state the

doctrine of the Trinity with any precision, although its roots are very clearly discernible. The leaders of the Church were quickly led to see, however, that there was no other form in which they could so adequately express and safeguard against misunderstanding the truth about himself that God had made known to them. In the words of the classic formula, God had revealed himself *as* the Father *through* the Son *in* the Holy Spirit. All three modes of the divine existence are clearly distinguishable and each has its own definite characteristics. There do appear to be three centers of personal unity in God. But, although they are distinguishable, they are not divisible. Each is fully God and yet One cannot be known without the Others. It is the one God with whom we have all the time to deal, as he makes himself visible in the face of Jesus Christ and becomes our contemporary in the Holy Spirit dwelling in our midst. So far, therefore, is the doctrine of the Trinity from being an idle and unimportant speculation that it could only have arisen among those who had known the God of Israel, and discovered that Jesus Christ was his Son, and who had experienced the fellowship of the Holy Spirit.

The Nature of God in Christ

Christians believe that it is here, in this series of events which culminate in Jesus Christ and the foundation of the Church, that we have the decisive revelation of God. It is through them, therefore, that we can learn most about the nature of this God. There are three characteristics in particular that stand out.

First, *God is a living God*. He is not an idea, but a Person, who enters into an active, responsive personal relation with his people. What we have in the Bible is not the account of how particular men studied the facts of their experience and came to the interesting conclusion that there must be a God

behind them. It is, on the contrary, the account of how particular men, who shared a community of experience, committed their lives to a Reality whom they could not evade and
who demonstrated, in events, that he had a continuing purpose
running through history. What is more, the faith of one man,
or of one generation, vindicated itself in the experience of another. The call of Moses led to the Exodus, the law, and the
settlement in the Promised Land. The expectation of the
prophets issued in the coming of the Messiah. God's conquer-
ing of the cross and tomb led to the resurrection faith of the
Church. The faithful proclamation of the universal gospel by
the apostles has led to the extension of the Church throughout
all the world. As men have walked along this way, new paths
have opened out to them. This supports the conclusion, as the
men of the Bible themselves saw, that their faith in God is
not mirage, but reality. God vindicates himself by his deeds,
by entering into history as an active, inescapable purpose. He
is the living God.

Secondly, *he is the universal God*. Theologians have learned
in modern times to speak of " the scandal of particularity " in
relation to the gospel. What they mean by this is that there is
something offensive to the mind of man in the fact that God
appears to speak his decisive word, not through general laws
discernible in nature and history, but in particular events and
persons, and events and persons in the life of an obscure nation
comparatively long ago. In the words of the popular jingle,
" How odd of God to choose the Jews! " It would indeed
be false to pretend that this fact does not raise difficulties for
all our minds. Yet, in the light of the nature and purpose of the
God revealed in this way, we can begin to see why God should
have acted through particular events. This is necessarily involved with the personal character of God and his dealings
with his children. He wishes to treat us, not as part of the

natural order, as objects, but as creative and responsible persons like himself. He has, therefore, to speak through and to particular individuals and groups of individuals and to do so through particular events. Yet what he says is of universal significance. Men of all kinds, wise and simple, rich and poor, in all kinds of societies and periods of history, are able to discover that this revelation speaks to their condition as nothing else does and performs in their lives the work that it claims to be able to do. Is it likely that they have all been deceived?

More than that, as we shall see more clearly in later sections, this revelation demonstrates its universality by placing the mysterious drama of human existence in the largest possible setting. Sin, death, and evil are given their full weight. Nowhere are they taken more seriously than they are in the Bible. And in that setting, a decisive and satisfying answer is given to their challenge. Out of a particular series of events in history, a light shines that illumines the meaning of all history, in terms which men of all kinds have been able to relate to their own experience.

Finally, *this God is " the Lord."* This became his title in the Old Testament, because his personal name " Yahweh " or " Jehovah " was too holy for men to take upon their lips. And it is this Lord who is personally present in Jesus Christ and no less present in the midst of his people as the Holy Spirit. This means that when he speaks and acts, what he says and does is not only universal in its reference but also decisive for mankind. There are many interesting and important questions about man and his world that the Bible does not raise or try to answer. One of the first principles of sound Biblical interpretation is not to look to it for answers to the wrong questions, as misguided sects are prone to do when they treat poems as scientific statements, or symbolic visions as predictions of modern history. But the question that the Bible does raise it answers in such a way as to make clear that here is the decisive answer of the ultimate Power, with whom all have in the last resort to deal, to the deepest question of the human spirit. The experience of salvation and reconciliation that Christ brings is one which, in its essence, cannot be superseded in this life by anything more important. New light can always break forth from it, and its complete fulfillment awaits the gathering together of all things in Christ, but when we have been truly laid hold of by it, we know that we are in the presence of the ultimate and decisive Power.

This is what Paul is making clear when he says at the end of the great eighth chapter of Romans that nothing " in all creation " is " able to separate us from the love of God in Christ Jesus our Lord." The meaning of revelation through the cross and the resurrection is that the challenge of that which held the strongest possibility of being able to dethrone God has been met and overcome. Nothing is able to come between him and us, for our Redeemer is the Lord.

At the heart of Christian teaching about God lies this testimony, made first in Scripture and confirmed in the experience of an innumerable company of believers in every age since the first: that the ultimate Power in the whole universe, on whom all else depends, has made himself known uniquely in Jesus Christ as a just and loving Father, who bears the consequences of human rebellion against him and imparts his own reconciling and renewing life to man, and who has promised to be with his children until the end of all things.

IS THE CHRISTIAN GOD AN ILLUSION?

A Perennial Question

How can we be sure that the Christian testimony which has just been described is valid?

The first point that must be made in trying to discover whether the Christian God has any real, independent existence, is that this is not a new question. All ages are disposed to exaggerate the novelty of their distinctive ideas and problems. It is true that, in many important respects, ours is an age unlike any that has happened before, and that we have many new experiences for which the past provides little guidance. But the basic human questions remain surprisingly similar from one generation to the next, even though the mode of their formulation may change; and it is only the superficiality of much modern education which could ever have led us to imagine otherwise.

In particular, it is essential that we rid ourselves of a certain arrogant sense of conscious superiority to our fathers which does more than anything to bedevil serious thinking about religious matters. The notion is widespread in Anglo-Saxon countries that our fathers (who for this purpose include everyone of a generation older than those who have this idea) were blessed with a commodity called " simple faith," which gave them a complacent and unruffled assurance that God was in heaven and that all was right with their world. This goes along with the other notion that this simple faith is denied to their children (ourselves) who are too clear-eyed, disillusioned, and experienced in the ways of the world to comfort themselves with such naïve illusions. It is a familiar attitude on the part of adolescents, who question beliefs for the first time, to assume that the possibility of doing so never occurred to their parents. Adolescents, however, are notoriously poor judges of their parents in such matters. Much of the so-called "doubt" of many people today has a curiously adolescent character, even when it is held by those who might reasonably be assumed to have reached maturity.

The truth is that, almost from the beginning, men have cast doubt on the reality of this God and of his purpose. Even after the Exodus and the exalted events associated with the giving of the law on Sinai, when these mighty happenings were fresh in their memory, the Children of Israel "murmured" against Moses and Aaron in the wilderness. They complained, "Would that we had died by the hand of the Lord in the land of Egypt, when we sat by the fleshpots and ate bread to the full; for you have brought us out into this wilderness to kill this whole assembly with hunger." (Ex. 16:2, 3.) It does not require much imagination to detect the sarcasm behind the reference to the hand of the Lord. What they are in effect saying is that they have been tricked by Moses and Aaron into following them on a wild-goose chase, and that there is no covenant, no Promised Land, and no overruling divine purpose.

Later in the history of Israel, we see that the psalms are full of challenges to God's reality. "The fool says in his heart, 'There is no God'" and "the fool" could there be translated, "the wise guy, who thinks he knows all the answers." The enemies of Israel, we are told, constantly mock them with the taunt, " Where is your God? " The psalmist himself, when he was hard-pressed and deeply troubled, cried out: " How can God know? And is there knowledge in the Most High? " The cast of mind of the men of Biblical times was such that they did not look out on the world as we do, with our scientific assumptions, and ask, " Do we see any evidences that lead us to belief in the divine existence? " God to them was someone essentially active, as we have seen, and what they always wanted to know was whether God was really at work. This ultimately is, however, the same question as ours. From this point of view we see that a book like Job, which appears chiefly concerned with the mystery of the sufferings of the righteous, is also concerned in its own way with a challenge to the reality of God.

The same thing is true when we come to consider the experience of Jesus himself. His faith was perfect or complete, but it was made complete through the things that he suffered, and part of his sufferings lay in his enduring the full onslaught of unbelief. It has already been suggested that the temptations should be thought of, not simply as the facing and rejection of inadequate ways of fulfilling God's will, but as a series of attacks by unbelief. And the experience of the cross means, not only the bearing of the burden of our guilt, but also the darkening of the face of God which is inseparably linked with the guilt. When the Creed speaks of Jesus' descent into hell, it refers to the liberation of the spirits imprisoned in the half-world that the Jews believed to be the abode of the departed, but that abode was conceived to be the place of meaninglessness and futility, where God did not dwell. We are meant to understand that by claiming for God that part of existence which was farthest away from him, and filling it with his divine life, Jesus took the full measure of unbelief and compelled it to do its worst. This is something beyond the capacity of the rest of us, for Christian experience teaches us that there is always something dishonest in our unbelief. Unbelief cannot, in the nature of the case, take itself with complete seriousness, for man cannot live without some kind of residual faith in God.

The experience of Jesus itself teaches us, therefore, that faith has always had to assert itself against its contradiction. Unbelief is not something peculiar to the modern world, either in extent or intensity. To see this is to see unbelief in its proper perspective. There is something slightly comic about the superior way in which people who have read a book by a Victorian scientist, or by a popular publicist like H. G. Wells, imagine that they have been emancipated from believing in the Christian God in a quite new and decisive way, when the reasons the scientist or publicist give for reaching this conclusion are actually far weaker than are the objections to belief in God with which the men of the Bible themselves were familiar.

This is not to say that modern times have not given a new urgency to some of the perennial objections to belief in God. But if it is clearly recognized that belief in God has always existed in victorious conflict with its contradiction, that fact in itself points us to one of the weightiest reasons in favor of the reality of the belief. At least, this seems to make clear that the Christian faith is not something that is accepted only because it is the conventional belief, which no one has the courage and independence of mind to challenge. On the contrary, it is a faith that has had to vindicate itself in the teeth of opposition from the outset, and which goes on being asserted with the deepest and most sincere conviction in periods when it is unfashionable, no less than in times when the climate of opinion is favorable.

Faith and Superstition

The word "illusion" was used in the title of this chapter largely because it is a popular modern word. A more precise word to describe what is meant when the word "illusion" is used in relation to the Christian faith would be the word "superstition." A superstition is a belief that arbitrarily asserts that something is true without being able to give any indication of why it should be or how experience demonstrates that it works out as being true. The characteristic of a superstition is that it cannot be explained rationally on its own premises. When it is explained rationally, it loses its point and power. It is arbitrary and capricious, something that has no clear reference either to morality or to rationality.

The contrast between this and Christian faith could not be greater. The response that God demands from man, which is what the New Testament means by faith, is the reverse of blind credulity. It is the unreserved commitment of the whole man, mind and heart and will, and that cannot be given unless he is genuinely convinced of the reality of that to which he commits himself. Jesus claimed to be the truth and therefore demanded that we accept him as the truth. The promise of the Holy Spirit is to lead us into the truth. All this is impossible if we do not test our faith to see whether it is true, in the way appropriate to the order of reality in which it exists. Anselm of Canterbury, the great theologian of the Middle Ages to whom reference has already been made, spoke of *fides quaerens intellectum,* "faith in search of understanding," and that has often been taken as a good definition of the task of theology. For it makes clear that the act of faith is of such a nature that it impels the believer to seek understanding in the sphere of his mind. This he cannot do without the most vigilant self-criticism and scrutiny of the object of his faith.

The Fruits of Faith

History, and not least recent history, provides abundant
evidence that Christian faith evokes this effort of understanding in a way in which a mere superstition could not possibly
do. It has been observed that Christianity is the only major
religion of the world that submits its sacred books to critical
examination. And it is important to note that it does this, not
for any propaganda purposes, but because its own nature is
such that it demands that it be done. It is still not widely
realized how much the science of Biblical criticism, as it arose
among Christians, influenced the general study of historical
documents in a scientific way, and helped to develop that
study's methods of work. In this, as in so many other ways,
the Christian faith itself taught the Church self-criticism. Indeed it can be said that if the notion of repentance, which is
central in Christianity, is given a wide enough connotation, it
is bound to lead men to a vigilantly self-critical attitude of
mind on the intellectual as well as on the moral level. Repentance prompts them to bring their whole lives, in all their parts,
under the scrutiny of the Word of God in Jesus Christ. Christianity cannot be mere superstition, because it is the proclamation of the forgiveness of sins and of a new start on the right
road, with guidance available to distinguish the right road
from the wrong.

This can be maintained without in any way minimizing the
fact that there is a dark side to the story of the Christian
Church, even on the intellectual level. Religious people have
often been and frequently still are bigoted and obscurantist in
the name of religion, not least of the Christian religion. Those
who write books extolling the virtues of so-called rationalism
delight to recount how Christian leaders have resisted the advance of science and have put barriers in the way of independ-

ent scrutiny of Christian truth because it has seemed to threaten their vested interest. Today we see people in some churches deliberately distorting the teaching of the Bible itself about race relations, because it suits them to do so.

This kind of thing has taken place, and no Christian interest can be served by denying the fact. What the critics of the churches do not always grasp, however, is that it is the natural tendency of *all* men, whether in the religious sphere or anywhere else, to resist new ideas when to accept them means a painful readjustment on their part. Charles Darwin, for example, incurred a good deal of odium from church leaders, but he incurred even more from his conservative scientific colleagues. It is not surprising that such an old-established body as the Church, the oldest institution with a continuous history in the modern world, should have many strong conservative tendencies. It is what history would lead one to expect. What is surprising is that, despite the weight of the past, there should be so much vigorous self-criticism, so much readiness to cast out cherished preconceptions and to take the initiative in venturing out in search of new truth. These characteristics are more apparent in some churches than in others, but there are few from which they are entirely absent. The rise of the modern scientific temper, which has often appeared to threaten the validity of Christian faith, probably owes much more to Christianity than some of its exponents appreciate. This scientific attitude learned from the Christian faith of the first scientists a belief in the rationality of the universe, and gained from them an ability to sit down patiently before the facts and not to manipulate them. Time and time again, Christianity has produced its own sternest moral and intellectual critics, and has emerged purified and renewed from their chastenings. It has produced in its adherents the power to be born again when they are old, the truest mark of divine activity. This is not what degrading and enervating superstitions do for their devotees.

The moral results produced by Christian faith are more commonly brought forward in justification of its truth than are the intellectual. This used to be the case particularly in the nineteenth century; and even today we frequently hear people say that, while they cannot accept Christian dogma, they recognize the validity of the Christian ethic. We have learned, however, to be more cautious than we used to be in using this kind of argument. The complacency with which it was sometimes put forward in Victorian times stands out the more clearly now that, in the course of the twentieth century, some of the weaknesses of the so-called Christian civilization of the West have stood so clearly revealed in two world wars. And in addressing the person whom our forefathers did not hesitate to describe as heathen, we have learned that he generally has his own religion and his own code of morals, which he sometimes obeys with a zeal that puts us to shame. We have learned through the encounter with those of other faiths that there is more in common between us in our humanity than we previously realized, and that it is that very truth which the God and Father of our Lord Jesus Christ has been teaching us through the encounter.

This " zeal of the pagans " is a fact, and attention still needs to be called to it in some Christian circles. But however the recognition of this fact may qualify our approach to religions and cultures other than our own, the moral results produced by Christian faith remain legitimate evidence against those, often themselves the products of Christian civilization, who dismiss Christianity as an outworn superstition. To put it on a very practical level, think of a feckless, self-righteous young student in a big city, who has already made a resounding mess of his personal relationships and the quality of whose academic work is visibly deteriorating as a result of his arrogance and drinking habits. Such people can sometimes be heard dismissing their hard-working, clean-living, churchgoing parents, who pinched and scraped to give them a good education, as the gullible slaves of outworn superstition. In such a situation the word " superstition " has been given a connotation the opposite of that which it has been accustomed to have in the history of human thought.

The story of the Christian Church has its dark side. This raises theological problems that we shall have to look at in the next chapter. Christianity, however, has never pretended that things would be otherwise, and on nothing is the Bible more insistent than that religion itself can go bad and become a source of corruption. The notion that all religion is a good thing, which is so widespread today, would never have occurred to the men of the Bible. But even the most assiduous muck-raking through the slums of Christian history cannot finally obscure the fact that with the Christian faith a new power has been born into the world, which transforms men's lives and produces the highest qualities of saintliness the world has ever seen, often out of the most unpromising material.

This may not be a conclusive argument in favor of the truth of the Christian claim, and it is not here put forward as such. It is put forward as evidence to suggest that, in contrast to the illusions that enslave men, there is something in belief in the Christian God which corresponds to fundamental reality. This belief does appear to have the ability so to organize the human constitution as to liberate powers within it which enable men to master and not to be mastered by life. Those overpopular books that describe this belief as " the power of positive thinking " or " the secret of victorious living " are not wrong in the claim they make for it. They are wrong only in the oversimplified account they give of how it achieves this end and of the trivialized conception they appear to have of the end. To put the point in more authentically Christian language, there is a good deal of evidence to support the claim that sin does indeed work death, and that the believer can do all things through Christ who strengthens him.

It used to be a favorite argument of those who took a non-Christian view of life that religion may have been a necessity in the childhood of the race, when men were not strong enough to face the shock of reality, and when they lacked the scientific techniques to master their environment. But now, as the argument goes, conditions are different. Truly emancipated modern men do not need the comfort and reassurance that religion provides. They are the masters of their fate and the captains of their souls.

Much can be said about this point of view. It is more than doubtful whether its reading of the attitude of mind of modern men is true, even if a certain pathos is given to the independence of modern man, alone with his anxieties. Where that independence has a positive quality, it can often be shown to stand in a surprisingly close relation to a vital Christian tradition, even by way of reaction. But whether such an account is a faithful reading of the condition of modern man or not, it is a demonstrably unfaithful account of the function that belief in the Christian God has performed in the history of mankind. This belief has brought with it an immense emancipation from the enslaving influence of false religion and has been the historical cause for the release of that buoyant, joyful ability to range throughout the whole of experience in freedom and without fear, which is the mark of the modern world at its best. The achievement of spiritual maturity, of full-grown manhood, is the purpose of the gifts of the Spirit that dwells in Christ's Church, as the fourth chapter of Ephesians indicates (Eph. 4:7-16). The modern world has yet to prove that it is possible to find the realism and independence it admires in any other way than through Christ. Experience suggests that to attempt to root this independence elsewhere leads only to a new enslavement to those demons of fear and ignorance and idolatry from which Christ delivers us.

Why Does Faith Sometimes Look Like Superstition?

It is worth asking why men ever came to accept an argument so obviously at variance with the facts as this which says that belief in the Christian God is superstition. They did so because, largely through the failure of the churches, the Christian faith seemed to many to lose its invigorating and adventurous quality, and public profession of it became the badge of social respectability. A tradesman who wanted customers or a family that aspired to improve its status had to be seen in church, and the right kind of church. This was not the whole story of late nineteenth-century religion of course. It achieved social success largely because of its strength and sincerity, but having achieved that success it was exposed to great dangers. These were that it should encourage conformity rather than self-criticism, superficiality in moral judgment, and a fear of innovation in thought and practice. When these attitudes were combined with the proper respect that should be shown each individual by the Church, it was inevitable that the conventional, timid, and unsuccessful should find the churches particularly appealing, precisely because the churches seemed to provide them with a refuge from a harsh world that they could not face.

When the hardly won knowledge produced by scientific discovery came to the notice of young minds, and when the opportunities for new experience provided by greater wealth and mobility were presented to them, it was natural that they should conclude that the life of the age had grown past the religion of the churches, and that salvation was now to be found in another direction. Sin seemed to them no longer to work death, but only a more interesting form of life. This was because sin had become identified in their minds with what the most timid members of society considered to be proper moralistic conduct in matters of secondary importance.

But experience has shown that the reaction against the tired faith of churchgoers was often nearly as superficial as that faith itself. The perils of even a justified spiritual protest are nearly always unavoidable unless the protesters are acutely aware of them. Sin, in the Bible's sense of man's self-centered rebellion against God, does work what looks very much like death; and modern men are increasingly coming to see that it is only by turning to the Lord Jesus Christ that they can find the power to achieve the moral renewal for which the world today cries out. The moral fruits of *authentic* faith indicate that this is not the kind of faith that is fostered by blind superstition.

Faith and Tragedy

There is another consideration which indicates that what is dealt with in the Christian story is reality and not illusion. It is one to which we have had occasion to call attention at several points in this discussion, but which has peculiar relevance in this instance. This consideration is that, so far from trying to avoid the dark and enigmatic side of human life, Christian faith faces it directly. Christian faith does not minimize the significance of sin and suffering and death. On the contrary, it takes them with far greater seriousness than does any other interpretation of life.

Much attention has been paid in recent thought to the tragic element in human life. Man is a creature who aspires after eternity and who has to die. He longs to create and to make his own the perfection of beauty; but in the act of enjoying it, its transitoriness comes home to him, and it eludes him. He is aware of an infinite moral constraint and aspiration, yet he finds himself constantly choosing only the lesser of two evils.

It is the mark of the Christian faith that it compels men who would prefer to forget these tragic facts to ponder upon their meaning. This is part of the message of the cross of Christ. And it is only when their significance is apprehended, and an interpretation of life is made that does justice to them, that the message of hope and promise is given. Christianity is not a modern funeral-parlor religion, which tries to pretend that death and all that goes with it does not really happen. It is the resurrection from the dead.

Reinhold Niebuhr entitled a well-known book of his sermons *Beyond Tragedy,* and that is a good description of the way in which living faith comes. Faith is a leap into the unknown and unfathomable, a casting off of all comforting human security, in which the believer discovers that God is real and is able to sustain men. It is itself a death, but a death that issues in new birth. And it is of the essence of that new birth that it is a discovery of the real world, with the clouds of illusion rolled away. "Though I was blind, now I see."

If therefore the Christian faith is to be dismissed as an illusion, the word "illusion" must be given a special meaning, and it must be an illusion on a level far more profound than that to which human experience normally probes. That it may still be an illusion is a possibility which the Christian must never shut out. However, as we have seen, it is his faith itself, rather than pressure from unbelievers, that compels him never to shut out that possibility. What can be said with confidence is that no one who denies the Christian faith has yet given an account of the whole mysterious story in such a way as to dissolve the mystery and demonstrate where and how the Christians have been deceived. Christian faith, after all, is one of the great events in the spiritual experience of the race. It needs to be worked over with knowledge, care, understanding, and attention to detail, if any fallacies are to be exposed. So far, it has to be recorded that no one has ever made the attempt in a way that cannot quickly be shown to be incompetent. No book written about the Bible has yet appeared which seriously challenges the faith of an honest and informed believer. No answer has yet been given by the human race to the question " What do you think of the Christ? " which stands up to full critical examination along the whole range of experience except that given by Peter in faith, " You are the Christ, the Son of the living God."

5

DOES EXPERIENCE VINDICATE FAITH IN GOD?

Difficulties Raised by Faith for Faith

How far have we come at this stage? We saw first of all that no one had the right to rule out the question of God's existence as unworthy of discussion, and that any truth arrived at in the realm of ultimate meanings had as much title to be considered as truth in any other realm. We reminded ourselves of the importance and the difficulty of a genuinely critical approach in dealing with matters of faith. We saw how the traditional rational proofs of God's existence raised questions but did not provide conclusive answers and that they could be seriously misleading by giving a wrong idea of the decision involved in faith in God. The question of God's existence must turn on that of whether he has himself taken the initiative in revealing himself to man. We looked at the story of God's self-revelation, which the Bible records, trying to recapture some of the mystery and startling uniqueness of that story, which can be dulled by its familiarity. Finally, we considered whether the experience of God, which Christians claim to receive through this revelation, could be dismissed as an illusion, and came to the conclusion that it could not.

This does not mean, however, that all obstacles to the faith of the Christian believer have been removed. On the contrary, faith means a venture into the unknown, and it is a venture that must be constantly made anew if faith is to be alive. Faith lives in constant tension with unbelief, as we have seen; and the assaults of unbelief take constantly new forms with developing experience. The Christian now lives in active communion with God the Father through Jesus Christ in the communion of the Holy Spirit. This greatly enlarges the scope of his life and leads him into situations and into difficulties he never knew before. His life is much richer than it was, but it is also more complicated. He has more expectations from life than when he lived in a world where he had little faith and hope. And what is true of the individual believer is no less true of the believing community and through it of the world in which the believing community is set and in which it has influence. "Love and suffering," it has been said, "create places in the heart that were not there before," and it is Christ above all others who teaches us to love and suffer. The result is that many difficulties about the reality of the Christian faith press more hardly on believers than they do on unbelievers, because it is only believers who have been led to a place where the difficulties arise.

Love and Suffering

The mention of the words "love" and "suffering" calls to mind the difficulty in regard to believing in the Christian God that is generally in the forefront of the attention of people today. How can a God whom we have learned to regard as loving permit so much suffering, and with it so much evil, in a world that he has made?

This is a question that is frequently discussed in these days and many excellent books are available which deal with it. Only a few comments can be made about the question here, and they are about aspects of it that are often overlooked. The first comment is a reminder of the curious fact that evil and suffering have become a serious difficulty to Christian believers only at a comparatively late stage in Christian history. The New Testament hardly discusses the problem at all. Suffering is certainly spoken of in the New Testament, and the men of the New Testament knew plenty of it, but they saw suffering as a test of their faith and an occasion for repentance and for anticipation of the glories of God's final reign. Even The Book of Job is not about the problem of suffering as we understand it today. It deals with the specific problem of why Job, God's righteous servant who almost certainly represents Israel, should know such misery and hardship.

This comes out no less vividly in the later history of the Church. The order for the visitation of the sick in the Episcopal *Book of Common Prayer* is a case in point. It is hard to imagine any minister daring to address a sick person in such terms on his own authority today, and most modern pastoral psychologists would have many hard things to say to him if he did. The order shows very little anxiety to reassure the sufferer of God's loving care, in case his affliction has made him doubt it. Rather, the occasion is used as a reminder to the sufferer that his end draws nigh and that there is time for penitence. Only after that has been made clear is much comfort given.

It has been more commonly observed that the problem of the suffering of the apparently innocent often worries those who have *not* suffered deeply more than those who have. Nothing is more unpleasant than the complacent religiosity that confronts the sufferer with the bland assurance that his sufferings are, after all, the will of God and have probably been sent to him because of his sins. But genuine Christian teaching about suffering does not arise in the same dimension as that in which the comforters of Job move. The Christian teaching was formed by those who knew what it was to suffer, and to suffer in the fulfillment of God's will. It is Job, and not his comforters, who cries in the end, " I had heard of thee by the hearing of the ear, but now my eye sees thee; therefore I despise myself, and repent in dust and ashes " (Job 42:5,6). It is our Lord himself who, as he gives up the ghost, cries, " Into thy hands I commit my spirit," a cry echoed, with joyful faith, by multitudes of his followers in their last agony. When Paul cried, " Who shall separate us from the love of Christ? " and listed a whole series of calamities, he was not being merely rhetorical. He was speaking as one who had known peril and nakedness and sword and who had yet discovered that in all these things we are more than conquerors through him that loved us (see Rom. 8:35–39). It was not smug insensitivity that prompted the authors of the *Book of Common Prayer* to phrase the order for the visitation of the sick in the way in which they did. It was rather the fact that those who have known the fellowship of Christ's sufferings have found in that fellowship a meaning that strengthens rather than weakens their faith in God. The authors of the prayer book knew that suffering was not due to the malignant caprice of God, but mysteriously to that deep rift between God and his creation which moves through the universe, of which sin is the expression in the moral sphere, and in which we are all involved. And they also knew that, deep though that rift is, it is not beyond the power of God to reach across it to sustain them and to exercise his healing grace.

The dilemma posed by suffering, that if God is all-loving he cannot be all-powerful and if all-powerful then not all-loving, is very hard to resolve on the level of thought. Yet it is resolved on the practical level in the experience of multitudes who suffer and yet rejoice in their Savior's praise, counting it a privilege to share with him a little of the burden he bore in seeking to bring back a world estranged from the source of its health and peace. To the outsider, who does not know the Lord Jesus Christ, this must always seem unconvincing. Even to the believer who has not himself been called to suffer much, this is a great mystery. Many of those who have been driven by suffering into the secret place of the Most High do insist, however, that there they abide under the shadow of the Almighty. Many of them find that suffering quickens their apprehension of reality, and they are able to find reassurance that God reigns and that he banishes the threat of meaninglessness, which is the deepest threat inherent in their suffering.

What is more, those who suffer in a Christian way know that what is true for themselves cannot be untrue even for those in whose sufferings the outsider can see little or no meaning and only cruelty — in, for example, the deaths of terror-stricken children caught by disaster or in the desperate agony of cancer. Those who suffer in a Christian way often learn from their sufferings that, although we cannot see the end from the beginning and there are many dark places in the way, we remain in the hands of God and that he can be peculiarly close to those who, like his Only-begotten Son in whom he was well pleased, are called upon to suffer.

Why then does this particular issue present itself so sharply to us today? It may be partly because we are genuinely more sensitive to suffering than former generations. That is certainly true on some levels. The immense extension of hospital facilities and our loving care for little children are a very sure indication of this. But it may also partly be because we possess a strong humanitarian sense, which was itself born of a religious upbringing, but which is not always allied to religious feeling in our own case. Declining faith often brings with it both a loss of moral robustness and oversensitivity to one's own and other people's feelings. A perverse form of this sensitivity is the attitude that combines great anxiety for the well-being of criminals and relative indifference to that of their victims.

That we should be so worried by the problem of God's love and suffering humanity does credit to our feelings, but the way in which we are worried by it suggests that we may not be as aware as we might be of all the factors that need to be taken into account in the situation. Perhaps the problem cannot be solved even on the provisional human level unless we learn to look at it in a different perspective. When we do, we may find that the Bible and classical theology are not so indifferent to the problem of suffering as might at first appear, but that they look at it in a more challenging and illuminating way.

The Christian Form of the Question

The form in which this question comes to the men of the New Testament is something like this. The message of the gospel is that Jesus Christ is risen from the dead. He has overthrown the enemies of God's purpose, and his Spirit is already present among men. When Jesus said, " The kingdom of God is within you," he did not mean simply that it was an internal spiritual Kingdom. He meant, The Kingdom of God is *in your midst*. Christ's servants, as Paul says, are able to destroy " every proud obstacle to the knowledge of God." Now it is true that the Bible never says that, once the Spirit of Christ has come, evil will immediately disappear. On the contrary, it speaks emphatically of the Christian life as a spiritual warfare against evil. Yet, even if that is granted, we cannot help wondering whether evil should be as strong as it so often appears to be in a world which God has made and where those who live by the Spirit possess his power. Does not the failure of the Church to live up to the first flush of Pentecost suggest that, after all, Christ was either deceived or else made excessive claims for himself? Is the Christian faith really more than a pious hope that good will somehow prove itself in the end to be stronger than evil?

It is questions like these that often lie behind the familiar statement, " Christianity is a fine ideal, but it doesn't work out in practice." But questions like these frequently arose in Scripture itself. The psalmists and the prophets had many occasions to doubt God's power. They were sustained by the hope that the day of the Lord would come when he would " judge the world with righteousness, and the peoples with his truth." According to Christian faith, that day came. Christ won salvation for us, and the powers of " the age to come," of God's eternal Kingdom dwelt in our midst. Yet from a very early time in the history of the Church, the problem raised by the apparent delay in the full coming of the Kingdom emerged. At the beginning, the apostolic writers give the impression that they were sustained by a conviction that the Lord would quickly come again and gather all things to himself. Later, there is more emphasis on the presence of the risen Christ in the Spirit, although there is no lack still of eager looking forward to the consummation of all things in him.

We shall see that this question of the apparent delay in the full coming of God's Kingdom is not only raised in the Bible, but also that an answer to it is given. This does not prevent it from recurring again and again in history, whenever people earnestly long for a consummation that they believe to be the will of God but which is denied them on this earth. That concern has received moving expression in a speech by Joan of Arc in Charles Péguy's play of that name, a speech that made a deep impression when it was performed in Paris during the German occupation in 1940: " O God, if only the beginning of your Kingdom would come. If only the sunrise of your Kingdom would come. But there is nothing, nothing to see, ever. You sent your Son, whom you loved so much, your Son came, who suffered so much, and he died and there is nothing, nothing ever. If only we could see the dawn of your Kingdom begin to break. And you sent your saints, and you called them each by name, and your saints came and nothing, nothing ever. Years went by, so many years that I do not know how many there were; centuries of years went by; fourteen centuries of Christendom, alas! since the birth and the death and the preaching. And nothing, nothing ever. And what reigns on the face of the earth is nothing, nothing, nothing but perdition. . . . God, God, can it be that your Son died in vain? That he came, and it was all for nothing? "

A similar point is made by that modern Judaism that is informed with a Biblical approach. It will not accept Jesus as the Messiah because, it alleges, he has not delivered Israel. The day of the Lord has not come and the world goes on in much the same way as it always has.

In answer to those who are baffled by the apparent delay in God's victory, it can be said first that they are generally tempted to overstate their case. This is obviously true in the quotation from Péguy, impressive in its way as it is; and it can also be shown to be true in regard to Judaism, although the terrible fate that has befallen so many Jews in our own time may make such overstatement understandable. But the world does *not* go its way as though Jesus Christ had never lived. Even on the level of recordable external events, which is far from being the most reliable source of evidence in a matter of this kind, it can be shown that the coming of Jesus Christ has made a greater difference to the history of mankind than any other event that has ever happened. If Judaism be seen as one special side of the same movement, it must be recognized that an entirely new dimension of experience and quality of life has come into the world with the coming of the movement that reaches its fulfillment in Jesus Christ.

Those of us who live in Western lands find it hard to realize what a transformation of the very assumptions under which life is lived has taken place under the influence of the Christian gospel. Very often, we fail to see how that gospel lies at the source of attitudes that now seem to go forward under their own momentum. A European theologian has remarked that he believes that the well-known activism of Americans is largely due to the fact that they believe, deep down inside themselves beneath the level of articulation, that the resurrection of Jesus Christ has really taken place and that now all things are possible. Whether that is true or not, it does indicate how deep-rooted Christian influence is on the whole mentality of many people in the Western world. Modern Christian romanticism has encouraged us to look for Christian influence only in spectacular and dramatic actions. It has made us overlook the fact that Christian influence may be at its most effective in the ordinary decencies and enlightenments that are taken for granted, but whose absence becomes quickly obvious when we move into a society into which they have not entered.

Yet this does not dispose of the whole difficulty. To use the language of the Old Testament, if there are signs that God's " hand is not shortened, that it cannot save," why are his judgments not more manifest in the earth?

It has already been suggested that the Bible has an answer to this question and it may help us to find our answer if we consider what it says. One reason for our difficulty is that the New Testament's way of looking at time is different from the way in which we normally think of time. The Bible not only looks at time chronologically, but also realistically. Two words are frequently used for time in the New Testament, *chronos* and *kairos*. *Chronos* is ordinary duration, in which moments succeed each other in a neutral, measurable chronological way, with one being much like the next. The word *kairos,* however, has the sense of "the fullness of time." It is an extension and development of the idea we have when we speak of "doing things at the right time." It is time infused with purpose, the time that makes history. That is why the coming of Christ is described as a *kairos*. It is the decisive event in history in this sense. It does not do away with ordinary chronological time, but it makes an all-important difference to what happens henceforward in chronological time, and makes us look at what happened in past chronological time in a different light.

We can put this in another way by saying that in the cross and resurrection of Christ the inner meaning of reality is unveiled for us. Sin, suffering, and death remain in the world, as they did before he came, but in the light of what he was and did we see that they do not have within them the power to overcome the love, goodness, and life of God. At the heart of the universe, evil has been overcome and in the coming of Jesus Christ this is made clear in the midst of the broken, ambiguous world in which we dwell. Our task is to register the victory of God in our lives together and in our dealings with the nonhuman world around us. We can do this in confidence because, with the apostle Paul, we now know that our labor is not in vain, is not likely to be useless and meaningless, in the purpose of God. We also look forward to the fulfillment of the victory we only partly register on this earth, when chronological time will be no more.

This helps to explain the two-sided character that the Christian life always has. It is a life of the fellowship of Christ's sufferings and of the power of his resurrection, and the one cannot properly be known without the other. Our lives on this earth are conformed to the cross and resurrection, and when we try to have one without the other we are misled. The power of sin is still active in our lives and we are caught in a network of sinful relationships. We are men of unclean lips who dwell in the midst of a people of unclean lips. Yet sufficient power is available to us even in this situation to overcome sin and to act in conformity with rather than against the will of God. God is in the midst of us in his Spirit, and the Spirit will lead us into all the truth — even in a world where lies crowd in upon us. This tension between faith and unbelief, between grace and sin, is present in the life of even the greatest saint. When it is seen that the Christian claim is not that we are perfect people living in a perfect world, but sinners who suffer and are glorified with Christ, our bewilderment about the apparent delay in the coming of Christ's Kingdom is diminished.

This is not to say, however, that there is no progress in the Christian life. The true Christian presses on, that he may attain the mark of his high calling, and he finds that, in doing so, God sustains him. He knows that the purpose behind the universe is not neutral, but on his side. That the Christian life possesses this progressive character is demonstrable from history, always provided that we remember what constitutes the relevant history in this matter. Spiritual progress is discernible only very imperfectly in terms of statistics or the life of the institutions, even though those institutions are dignified with the titles of churches. It is measured primarily in terms of the internal life of believers. When we remember that, it becomes notable that only rarely do people who build their lives firmly on a Christian foundation collapse and lose their faith. Evil and its power may never be finally vanquished in their lives, but the grip of evil seems progressively to weaken. Those in whom the good work of Christ is truly begun find that sufficient resources are available to complete it.

Progress does exist in the Christian life. But we need to remember that there is progress in evil also. Jesus tells us that the good and the evil grow together unto the Day of Judgment. Just as the good, by which we here mean the dynamic will of God, develops according to its own inherent logic, so does the evil, which is the contradiction of his will. The Christian will understand why good and evil should grow together, because the presence of the good will cause the evil to show its fury at its most venomous. The warmth of the Sun of Righteousness draws out its essential nature, in the same way as it does the good. The cross of Christ demonstrated this once for all. Evil in lands where the gospel has long been preached, and has had a strong formative influence upon men's lives, is nearly always more savage, hysterical, and cruel, and burns itself out more quickly, than in lands where men have not been stabbed by the gospel into a high degree of self-consciousness.

This is another way of suggesting that there is a day of judgment. The Day of Judgment is an aspect of the Christian faith that has been slurred over by many churches in recent times, but which is coming to be emphasized afresh in the strenuous days in which we live. It is not always clear from Jesus' teaching about judgment whether he is referring to his own cross and resurrection or to a final event toward which they point. The probability is that he refers to both, with the cross and resurrection as a decisive revelation of the final realities, to which, however, they point forward as their consummation. The reality of eternal life, which will stand and not be destroyed in the judgment, is made clear in Christ, but it is a reality experienced still in a world shot through with sin and therefore which is known only in the act of faith that overcomes the power of sin. Yet the nature of that reality is such that it points us forward to a state of life when we shall know it in a different way. When that comes, God's victorious power will not need to express itself through struggle with its contradiction, which is evil. We shall know eternal life, without the imperfection and impoverishment that we always experience on this earth. The Spirit will not be the first installment of our inheritance but its fullness. And when that happens, all that belongs to " this body of death " will be judged and condemned.

When this Day of the Lord will be, we are not told. In fact, modern dissatisfaction with the imperfect images in which the New Testament tries to express the life to come has concealed from us the fact that, at its most characteristic, the New Testament is exceptionally reserved about this whole matter. To inquire after times and seasons is to misunderstand the realities with which we are here dealing, and to expose oneself to the rebuke administered to those who seek for signs. The reality of this other life, however, presses upon us at every stage of this present life, whether we are conscious of it or not. The Early Church's way of speaking of the Day of the Lord as being imminent may have been misleading on one level, but it was not basically wrong. It was a way of expressing, perhaps in excessively chronological terms, an ever-present reality as a factor that could never safely be left out of account. The pious Evangelical custom of writing *D.V.* (*Deo volente*), or " God willing," after notices of meetings is exposed to the characteristic danger of smugness, but it is not in principle wrong. It is at one with the essential spirit of the New Testament.

Nothing is farther from the truth than the notion that the preoccupation of the New Testament with the " last things," what is called " eschatology," weakens our concern for Christian action in this life. On the contrary, it gives greater urgency to what we do here and now. Men are to live now by the Spirit, as children of the light and of the day, inspiring this passing world with the power of the eternal world, that they may be found doing his business by the Lord when he comes. The

men of the New Testament saw the Church as the community
of the interval between the times of our reconciliation to God
in Christ and of his final victory, but it is a community that
busily reclaims this passing world for Christ, while at the same
time waits to "put on . . . [its] heavenly dwelling" (II Cor.
5:2).

Why Should There Be Continuing Evil?

When the history of Christian experience since our Lord's
day is considered in this light, it is easier to see the ways in
which Christian faith vindicates itself in history. It is vain to
pretend, however, that we can explain why evil should continue
to exist in the world. To say that it is due to man's free will
may emphasize the element of human responsibility for much
evil, but this does little more than push the problem one stage
farther back. Is the possibility of choosing evil necessary to the
choice of good? We are here, once more, in the realm of mystery, but of mystery in which meaning can be seen, meaning
that further enhances the mystery. Indeed, it must be said that,
next to the mystery of grace, the mystery of evil, of " iniquity "
as the Old Testament calls it, is the ultimate one. Why such a
thing should be in a world that a loving God has made is, in
the nature of the case, inexplicable. It is irrational, absurd. If it
were possible to fathom this mystery, evil would cease to exist.
Perhaps one aspect of eternal life will be that while the mystery
of God will remain, evil will be exposed in its full hollowness
of irrationality and in so doing will vanish. Our knowledge of
evil comes out of the same dimension as our knowledge of
God, and the act of faith is an insight into the nature of final
reality, which sees the ultimate vanity of evil.

While we remain men in this world we cannot fathom the
whole depth of this mystery but this, at least, can be said. Evil
may still present itself as a reality, but the power of the risen

Christ in the Spirit is certainly no less of a reality and, in its constantly renewed encounters with evil, proves its greater strength and durability. God's Spirit is at work in the world and, when it truly breaks forth, the evil spirits cower in terror and flee. This is true, not only of moral evil but also of meaninglessness, the elements in life that make no sense. When the light of God shines upon these things, we know that it is the only power that can bring order and coherence into them. It is true that there are many questions whose answers are not given us, but the unanimous testimony of Christian experience is that we do know the answer to Socrates' fundamental question, "How shall a man live?" and can obey his exhortation, "Know thyself." Darkness still exists, but the light does shine in it and the darkness is unable to comprehend it. We have the Spirit of Christ, and that Spirit convicts us of sin and leads us to righteousness and shows us the truth with sufficient clarity to enable us to await our Lord's final appearing in his own good time with confidence and hope, a hope sure and steadfast, and one which enters into that which is veiled.

Is the Christian God the God for All Men?

The Case for Agnosticism

It might be agreed that our discussion has, at least, proved the point made at the outset, that the question concerning the reality of God is not one that anyone can dismiss out of hand. It proves worthy of more attention than most people give to it. At the same time, the discussion has at several places indicated an awareness that there is a case against as well as a case for. On no matter are men more sharply divided than this. Is it not best to keep an open mind upon it? Arrogant atheism may be without excuse, but is not an attitude of agnosticism, which may show grateful respect to the Christian tradition but which says that it does not know, admissible and even respectable?

We all know that this is a common attitude today. America differs from a country like Britain in that far more people would be prepared to assert in America that to them belief in God was self-evident, but it is doubtful whether the difference is in reality as great as statistics suggest. It is well known that the number of self-confessed and strong-minded atheists in the English-speaking countries is very small. In Britain recent studies by " Mass Observation," a public-opinion poll, suggest that very few even of the large number of people who do not

go to church confess to no faith in any kind of God. And a recent *Catholic Digest* survey of religious opinion in the United
States derived great comfort from the conclusion that 98 per
cent of those consulted said that they believed in God. Yet the
kind of God many of these people say they believe in is very
different from the God of the Bible. They often imagine someone vague, remote, and comparatively harmless, concerning
whose reality differences of opinion may be permitted because
he clearly does not affect the serious business of living in any
significant way. They feel that we are all entitled to speculate
about God, and, since this is a free country, each man's opinion
is as good as the next. This attitude has crept even into the
churches and some church people have made God over into
their own well-intentioned, confused and easygoing image.
Their God is an " optional God," and if some people find it
inconvenient to take up the option that is regrettable but not
decisive.

Two considerations of greater weight reinforce this apparently sensible attitude. The first is one we have already glanced
at. There are other gods than the God Christians call Father,
gods who are followed with a devotion and zeal at least super-
ficially comparable with that of Christians at their best. How
can we be sure that the Christian way is better than that of
Islam or the loftier forms of Buddhism? We were at great
pains to insist, in Chapter 3, that it is hard to know from the
outside what these rival faiths teach, and that we should be
careful not to make sweeping generalizations about their relation to Christianity. But does not this confirm the point? It is
difficult to decide this matter, and surely it is unreasonable to
expect those who have to get on with the business of living to
make up their minds. Is it not best to have an attitude like
some British colonial administrators, who treat all religions
with official respect and private detachment, and who are pre-

pared to regard the Christian missionary as a nuisance as great
as the fanatical Moslem or the witch doctor or the Communist
agitator as soon as he becomes administratively awkward about
his religion?

The other consideration that would seem to favor agnosticism is one that comes more often to the notice of ordinary
people. It is that there are many people who seem to get along
without conscious belief in God, and there are others who find
it hard to convince themselves that he exists. A great many
people, even in nominally Christian countries, seem to live
without giving more than an occasional thought to the whole
matter of religion. God no longer appears to be a significant
factor in their lives. Yet they are often decent and even likeable
people, occasionally more so than eager churchgoers. They may
have their faults, but don't we all? Their attitude of indifference is closely parallel to the bewilderment that better educated
and more self-conscious people express in relation to belief in
God. Their attitude suggests that belief does not pose a fundamental question that must be answered if man is to discover
his true nature. This in turn implies that the God who is the
object of such faith cannot be all that is claimed for him. He is
not the universal God, with whom all men have in the end to
deal. He is but one of the options presented to man trying to
make sense of his experience. Another option may, therefore,
turn out to be more acceptable. The right attitude of the man
of integrity toward God is surely one of reserve and agnosticism, which may be wistful or cynical according as his experience of the Church has been pleasant or otherwise.

The Necessity for Decision

These difficulties, which are widespread, can be met only by
a reconsideration of Christian experience itself. When that is

done it becomes clear that, whatever weight is given to these difficulties, those who have known Christian experience are emphatic that the nature of that experience is such as to compel decision. The Christian, as we have seen, does well to be agnostic about many matters, but not about the fundamental one. Indeed, one of the characteristics of Christian experience has been its ability to force decision upon those who would prefer to avoid it. Faith is always found in tension with unbelief, but perhaps the most characteristic manifestation of unbelief is a temporizing indecision in the face of the Christian claim. Men have always preferred to avoid making up their minds about God rather than to do anything so self-committing as to deny him outright. They have reserved their greatest resentment for those who have driven them into a situation where they had to make up their minds. This was the persistent complaint of the prophets in old Israel. " How long will you go limping with two different opinions? If the Lord is God, follow him; but if Baal, then follow him," and Israel eagerly seized any opportunity to limp between two opinions. When Jesus came, he came as one who compelled decision. " He who is not with me is against me." He cannot be put off until a more convenient season, as men discovered when they were left with no alternative but to crucify him. It is part of the distinctiveness of Christian experience that it exposes as illusory the notion that agnosticism about God's existence is a tenable position.

The chief reason for this is that no one can have even the faintest understanding of the Christian experience without realizing that in this matter the initiative lies with God and not with ourselves. This is the insight that is always denied to the person who tries to stand outside the situation, but which is always luminously clear to him who stands within. To use the language of theology, God is transcendent. Now this does not mean, as is erroneously imagined, " remote " or " far above us." What it does mean is " over against us." God is the other party to a personal encounter and in seeking to know him we do not look into the depths of our self-consciousness. We look outside ourselves as to another person, who is different from us and who depends upon himself and not upon us for his existence. He is not the projection of our own desires or sense of significance, nor can he be called up or dismissed according to our inclination. Christians speak of God as the " Lord " and this is part of what they mean by the term. It also helps to make sense of the otherwise puzzling notion of election, the belief that Christians have that they are each individually called according to his purpose. Whatever difficulties the notion of election may hold for our minds, at least it tries to describe a genuine element of Christian experience, that we have not chosen him but that he has chosen us. To think otherwise is to be thinking of someone other than the God whom Christians know.

The agnostic is, therefore, in the same position as the unbeliever. He is denying the reality of God the Lord, since to suppose that a noncommittal attitude toward God is possible means that he does not genuinely believe that the living God, the Lord, exists. Agnostics are, in fact, dishonest. They may resent the imputation, since it is often characteristic of people in this position that they believe themselves to be prompted by a peculiarly high standard of intellectual integrity; but if God be God, men cannot live and remain indifferent to him.

This is more obvious on the level of behavior than on the level of thought. If a man cannot make up his mind about God's existence, he cannot really answer the question " How shall a man live? " Whatever he may say, his actions show that he has answered that question one way or another. Some people try to maintain that morals do not seem to bear much relation to religious belief, but they can quickly be convicted of superficiality. Many people in the last couple of generations have tried to believe that patterns of moral conduct that were formulated in the light of the Christian belief in God, or received their fulfillment and sanction through that belief, are now able to stand in their own right. The Christians who were assumed to be hopelessly misled in theology were held to have been substantially right about morals. Such a position, unlikely on the face of it, has been shown by the events of the last forty years to have been the product of wishful thinking on the part of those who were more the heirs of a Christian heritage than they realized. Up to a point, kindness and tolerance and charity shine by the light that they carry within themselves, but they carry no compelling obligation for the unregenerate spirit of man unless he is brought to believe that they are the will of the ultimate Power to whom he will one day be answerable for his deeds. The rise of Communism and Fascism are only the most crudely vivid reminders to us that by itself a merely humanistic faith presents no barrier to the imperious demands of arrogant self-interest.

The truth is that many people of " good will " in the modern world who allege that they deny the Christian God do so only with the surface of their minds. Their basic attitudes are still conformed to a living faith, as often becomes clear in a real crisis. They are disciples who said, " I go not " and went, just as those churchgoers whose actions deny their professions are disciples of the other kind. Their own confusion of mind, or perhaps the unsatisfactory nature of the churches they know, prevents them from acknowledging their own basic decisions in relation to God.

But are the two considerations brought forward at the beginning of this chapter really met by the account of decision that has just been given? About the first of these, the matter of the conflicting testimony of the various world religions, this at least can be said. The point that the testimony of the world religions seems to be contradictory is made more often by those who are trying to *minimize* the importance of the religious issue than by those who are trying genuinely to relate these religions to each other. Those who study religions most closely are those who emphasize how much they differ from each other, and how necessary it is to reach some decision about the conflicting character of their claims. None of them, except possibly some forms of Confucianism, give much countenance to the agnostic attitude; for all of them believe that the dimension of religious experience is of supreme importance, and that decision is called for. Whatever the ultimate relation of the differing religions to each other may be, their comparative study serves only to sharpen the issue concerning the truth or the falsity of the claims of the Christian faith.

But what is to be said about the second argument for agnosticism — that there are many who are content to remain indifferent and many who find belief in the Christian God impossibly hard? Are they right and are believers wrong? First of all, many of the people of this kind who appear to be leading reasonably happy and worth-while lives are living, as Christian apologists are often quick to point out, on the Christian capital of former generations. This is a capital that is to be found not only in their environment, but also within their own personalities — in their attitudes, habits, and expectations of life. They are, in John Baillie's phrase, " men of the afterglow," whose lives still reflect the radiance of the Sun of Righteousness, even though they may believe that as far as they are concerned that Sun has set.

Now I have to admit that, if I were someone in that position, I could easily be irritated by being described in such a fashion by a Christian, especially if it were done in a complacent or pitying manner. Something more needs to be said, therefore.

This is a point at which Western Christians do particularly well to remember that they are men of like nature with their neighbors, who belong to the same culture, and that both the belief and the unbelief of this age have more in common with each other than might at first be apparent. We Christians are ourselves too much men of the afterglow and too much dependent on the faith of our fathers to feel very much different from our neighbors who do not confess Christ. Their open profession of indifference or unbelief should prompt us to inquire whether they are not articulating more clearly thoughts that are in our minds, and also whether it is not the feebleness of our own witness that confirms nonbelievers in their indifference or hostility.

At the same time, there are at least three considerations that may help us to conclude that this indifference and unbelief do not in themselves constitute a fundamental challenge to faith.

First, most of the indifferent and unbelieving are not in the position of having tried the life of faith and found it wanting. Their trouble is that they show little sign of having ever considered it seriously. We have seen how often this is true on the intellectual level, where few efforts have been made to reject the Christian faith on the basis of a reasoned and competent study of its claim. It is no less true on the ordinary level of everyday experience. It is not unfair to say, as a broad generalization, that most irreligious people are superficial people. And much of the apparent success in life that some of them achieve can be directly traced to their very irresponsibility. They have lightened their psychological load and have made a tacit agreement with themselves and with each other never to penetrate beyond certain levels of experience. Sometimes this attitude may be combined with a tolerant respect for religion. Occasionally, it even appears in the guise of a religion of " peace of

mind " and freedom from anxiety about any fundamental question. The busy social life of some communities operates on this
basis, and many clubs and a few churches exist as semiconscious
conspiracies to keep only to safe subjects and to gang up on
anyone who tries to penetrate into the dangerous realm of mystery where living faith becomes a possibility.

People who live in this way are good fellows enough, within
the framework of their little world, and provide ideal models
for cereal advertisements. They are often generous and open-
handed, provided they are caught in the right mood and no
sustained and disciplined sacrifice is required of them. They
are cheerful in minor adversity, provided they are not required
to take command. They have given up their high calling as
children of God, who enjoy the glorious liberty of his universe,
and have settled for being considered regular guys by their
fellows. In a society with a Christian leaven, they are harmless
and, if they have a good dress sense, can look decorative. In a
society governed by the strong and the ruthless, like Nazi Ger-
many or Communist Russia, they give no trouble.

If it be protested that although this may be true of the super-
ficially indifferent, it is grotesquely untrue of the liberal-minded
agnostic who has genuine intellectual difficulties about the
Christian faith, the question must be raised whether that is
entirely so. It is true that some people who are unable to commit themselves to Christian faith may have more affinity with
the genuine reserve of the Bible than do those overconfident
Christians who know all the answers before they have faced
any of the questions. Yet it cannot be without significance that
there is a certain indecisiveness of outlook, a temporizing habit,
about the whole mentality of the typical intellectual agnostic.
He is always seeking, never arriving at, the truth, in such a
way that a suspicion is raised that he may be more interested
in his own reputation as a man of independent thought and

proper feeling than in discovering the truth.

Secondly, it is a fair question to ask whether these people, the indifferent and the uncommitted, show any sign of having uncovered an interpretation of reality more profound and all-embracing than the Christian one. After all, the fact that the number of those who confess to uncertainty about Christian truth today is large has little relevance unless it can be shown that they have called attention to some great element in the human situation which Christians have overlooked and which exposes the vanity of Christian pretensions. Has this happened? We have seen that reserve about the life of some of the churches may be a sign of health rather than the opposite these days, but that is not the same as reserve about ultimate Christian truth itself. Have the uncommitted found some god who is stronger and more worthy of adoration than the God we know in Christ, even though he may be none other than man itself? Is their creed of not-knowing anything more than an attempt to live in a spiritual vacuum, which human — no less than physical — nature abhors? " Is there a God besides me? . . . I know not any," said the author of the later Isaiah in relation to the idols of his own day, and there has still been no effective rejoinder to him. How do these agnostics answer the charge that they are self-contradictory, living by powers they refuse to acknowledge or else giving up the attempt to live as real men at all?

Thirdly, it is a good rule not to take modern agnosticism too much at its own valuation of itself. What these people say with their lips is not necessarily what they believe in their hearts. Once a man takes a position publicly, even if it is an agnostic position, he develops a vested interest in it and will not readily reveal his private misgivings about it. This does not mean that we must not, as believers, take with full serious-ness those difficulties which agnostics do express. As we have seen, we can learn a great deal from them about our own difficulties. But we shall not assume that they tell the whole story, even about those who express them. Nor will we forget that they are men of like nature and like environment to ourselves, and that the issues between faith and unbelief are unlikely to present themselves to them in a way that is basically different from that in which they present themselves to us.

This is why the question of agnosticism and belief is best answered finally by each man for himself, in terms of his own experience. It is only partly true that every man is an island. It is more true that every man is a microcosm of humanity. If a man has the grace to recognize that the experience of others will help him interpret his own, he can confidently believe that the way in which the issue between God and men presents itself to him is likely to be the way in which it presents itself to other men also. We are members one of another even, and perhaps especially, in our relation to the living God. We should all know how possible it is to deny God or to be indifferent to him, because we are constantly tempted to do these very things ourselves. We know how easy it is to drift into a position of so-called agnosticism, in our hearts if not with our lips, because we are too lazy or too timid honestly to face the difficulties that faith presents to our thought. Once again, the devil's chief way of undermining faith is by distracting attention from the whole subject; and it is not faith but unbelief that makes us avert our attention from the difficulties involved in faith. Yet we know also that we could never have been brought to conviction about the Christian faith unless we had seen that the essence of belief was that God was a reality who was independent of us and who refused to allow us to have him on any terms except his own. The fact that the way to faith is through repentance and new birth, which cannot be counterfeited, is the surest sign that faith is no illusion and that it is God who holds the initiative in this matter.

What can those who have the gift of faith do to convince others of God's reality? It is of peculiar importance at this stage of the Church's history to see that the best and most effective way of doing this is to try to be honestly convinced ourselves. There is, of course, a place for deliberate efforts at evangelism, and many Christians need to do more of such evangelism; but to strain to convince our neighbors at any price or by any method is to give the impression that God is our servant and not we his, and thus to give the most seriously misleading impression possible of his nature. He has placed us in a world of mystery, where the answers to life's questions are not obvious. This means that we should not cheapen holy things, nor take his name too lightly on our lips, nor forget how costly, dangerous, and rewarding a gift faith is. Dogmas are necessities of mature Christian faith; but a dogmatic temper, even in evangelism, is ruled out by the nature of the realities with which we have to deal.

What God requires of his children, therefore, is not that they busy themselves overanxiously with justifying him before men, as though his ability to commend himself depended entirely on their salesmanship, but that they give him the humble obedience of their own hearts. That in its turn means that they believe his claim to be the truth and do not rest until they discover him, through the mists of doubt and uncertainty, to be the truth ever and anew. God is stronger than all that denies him, even stronger than the unbelief of the children he has made in his image. That is something we discover when we ourselves receive the gift of faith. We do so because God in his mercy has not taken us with final seriousness in our unbelief. If we testify to him out of our own experience, and show his reality in our lives, and maintain the ministry of intercessory prayer, we are doing all that he asks of us. He can use our witness in his own way to speak to our neighbors, and we shall not be hindering him in the expression toward them of his patience and mercy and truth and love.

BELIEVING IN GOD

Mr. Jenkins claims it has never really been easy for man to believe in God. However, some response to his reality and authority is inescapable. Ultimate dependence upon him may be affirmed or denied, but it can be neither proved nor avoided. In a time characterized by superficial belief and superficial unbelief it is especially important that men be challenged to face afresh the mysteries of their existence. This book can provide such a challenge. Its use can aid the conviction that for our time asking right questions may be more provident than giving neat answers.

QUESTIONS FOR DISCUSSION

Discussion I. Chapter 1. "Why Is Belief in God So Difficult?"

1. Why do some people say that belief in God is more difficult for modern man than for primitive man? Why does the author somewhat disagree?
2. Why are mystery and meaning interrelated? What is the difference between magic and mystery?
3. If "God is truth," why can we not understand him completely?
4. If it is not the business of theology to explain away the mysteries of life, then what is the function of theology?
5. In the depth of one's life, can Christ be accepted as Lord simply "on authority"? What forms does religious authority take?
6. Is that person a "better" Christian who sees every bush afire with God?
7. In what ways does the pure scientist depend on a kind of "faith" (unproved assumptions)?
8. Can the "scientific method" give us any help when we ask basic questions about the meaning of life?

Discussion II. Chapter 2. "Can We Prove that God Exists?"

1. What are the best known traditional proofs for the existence of God? How might a nonbeliever react to the traditional proofs?
2. What are the weaknesses and strengths in the moral argument for the existence of God?
3. How does the ontological proof differ from the other proofs?
4. Why is excessive emphasis on the traditional proofs misleading?
5. How is the question of God's existence more embracing than other questions about which we may speculate?
6. What are the two meanings of the word "reason"?
7. How does a person's faith (Christian or other) affect his reason?
8. From what sources does evidence that forces us to question our own sincerity come?

Discussion III. Chapter 3. "God in Jesus Christ."

1. Why do Christians turn to the Bible?
2. Why should we not think of Jesus "simply as an isolated figure"?
3. What has Biblical scholarship led us to understand as "the first sign of God's *historical* activity"? In what way then are the Genesis creation accounts to be appreciated?
4. What are the events by which the Old Testament is dominated?
5. Briefly, what characterized the behavior of the Israelites after they settled in the Promised Land? With what message did the prophets respond to this behavior?
6. How should we interpret Jesus' temptations?
7. Why were the apostles not necessarily interested in "proving" that the crucified Jesus had been seen alive?

8. Why does P. T. Forsyth say that Christ's "cross, resurrection, and glory" created the church?

9. If the doctrine of the Trinity is not stated as such in the New Testament, why has it been so important in the history of the church?

Discussion IV. Chapter 4. "Is the Christian God an Illusion?"

1. Was the religion of former generations a "simple faith"?

2. In what ways did Jesus have difficulty believing in God?

3. What is the difference between Christian faith and superstition?

4. What does the modern scientific temper owe to the Christian faith?

5. What dangers are there in citing Christian morality as evidence for the validity of Christian faith?

6. What can be bad about religion?

7. In what ways are the "positive thinking" books wrong? In what way are they right?

8. What happened after the nineteenth-century church achieved social success?

9. What does Mr. Jenkins suggest as a reason for modern young people's disinterest in the church?

10. Why can the Christian never completely shut out the possibility that Christian faith is an illusion?

Discussion V. Chapter 5. "Does Experience Vindicate Faith in God?"

1. Why does the author say that believers are likely to have more difficulty about the reality of the Christian faith than nonbelievers?

2. Why does suffering not produce doubt in the New Testament man?

3. On what level does the Christian resolve the old dilemma, How can God be all-loving and all-powerful in a world of suffering?

4. How does the way we think of time affect our interpretation of suffering?

5. Is there any progress in the Christian life? in the coming of the Kingdom? in evil?

6. How were the New Testament authors who spoke of the imminent character of the Judgment Day really correct?

7. In responding creatively to the conditions that evil causes, how is the Christian also responding to the questions that evil raises?

Discussion VI. Chapter 6. "Is the Christian God the God for All Men?"

1. For what reasons might agnosticism be better than belief in a God?

2. What does it mean to say that God is transcendent?

3. In what way does the author claim agnostics are dishonest?

4. Why is it impossible to postpone making a decision for or against the Christian God?

5. What is meant by "men of the afterglow"?

6. What are the reasons that contemporary religious indifference may not constitute a fundamental challenge to faith?

7. How might serious reflection on the agnostic claims aid a Christian?

8. What are some of the dangers in a "straining" evangelism?

9. How shall we make most effective witness to the Biblical God?

Suggestions for Discussion

The book divides quite naturally in two ways. If six discussions are contemplated, discuss one chapter at each meeting. To cover the book in four meetings, discuss first Chs. 1 and 2; secondly, Ch. 3 (with review of previous session); thirdly, Chs. 4 and 5; fourthly, Ch. 6 (with review of the preceding discussion).

This Study Guide was prepared by David W. McShane, director, Westminster Foundation of Philadelphia, Pa.